SAVE MONEY **GOOD FOOD**

Family feasts for a fiver

SAVE MONEY GOOD FOOD

Family feasts for a fiver

ROB ALLISON

Foreword by **Susanna Reid & Matt Tebbutt**

HODDER &
STOUGHTON

First published in Great Britain in 2017 by Hodder & Stoughton
An Hachette UK company

1

Save Money: Good Food Series Recipes and Foreword copyright © Crackit
Productions Ltd 2017
Additional Book Recipes and Text copyright © Crackit Productions Ltd
and Hodder & Stoughton Ltd 2017
Design and Photography copyright © Hodder & Stoughton Ltd 2017

A CIP catalogue record for this title is available from the British Library

Hardback ISBN 978 1 473 66272 8
eBook ISBN 978 1 473 66273 5

Editorial Director: Nicky Ross
Project Editor: Jo Roberts-Miller
Design and art direction: Smith & Gilmour

Recipes: Rob Allison
Photography: Dan Jones
Prop styling: Morag Farquhar
Food styling: Pip Spence

Colour origination by Born Group
Printed and bound in Germany by Mohn Media GmbH

Hodder & Stoughton policy is to use papers that are natural, renewable
and recyclable products and made from wood grown in sustainable forests.
The logging and manufacturing processes are expected to conform to the
environmental regulations of the country of origin.

Hodder & Stoughton Ltd
Carmelite House
50 Victoria Embankment
London
EC4Y 0DZ
www.hodder.co.uk

CONTENTS

Forewords by Susanna Reid
and Matt Tebbutt 7

INTRODUCTION 11

SPEEDY SUPPERS 25

FAMILY FAVOURITES 59

LEFTOVERS &
STORE CUPBOARD 117

FRIDAY NIGHT FEASTS 147

SOMETHING SWEET 193

Index 216
Acknowledgements 224

Who doesn't want to eat good food while saving money?

Like many busy parents, I often make the mistake of cooking the same few meals on an endless loop, ordering the same shopping list online without double checking the prices or my cupboards, and looking at leftovers with a heavy heart, knowing they'll hang about in the fridge before going in the bin. I knew I could save money AND food – I just needed some fresh, exciting ideas about what to cook for the family in order to keep them happy and healthy.

Matt and Rob have reinvigorated my attitude to the kitchen and revolutionised my weekly shop. I've learned how to whip up nutritious, tasty meals for the whole family from what is lurking unused in my cupboards, adding a few of the veg that were otherwise destined to be thrown away.

Too much of what we buy we don't use – either because we forget we have it or we don't know what to do with it. By using the recipes and ideas in this book, those forgotten fruit and veg will find their way into soups and stews, be used up as tasty pizza toppings, or cooked in batches and kept in the freezer for when you need a quick meal in a hurry.

Frightened by Best Before deadlines and confused about how long you can keep fresh food or when it needs to be chucked? Matt and Rob will cure you of your Best Before phobia and clarify the rules.

Stuck in a rut of chicken and sausages every other day? These recipes will encourage you to use different cuts and add flavours and fillings to transform meals that have become dull and repetitive. They'll help you break your habits and use different, cheaper cuts of meat and enable you to create meals at home to rival the pre-prepared meals and takeaways that may be costing you more than you think.

I'm now having more fun in the kitchen, cooking better meals with more variety and saving money while I do it. What a delicious result!

SUSANNA REID

Knowing how to cook will help you save money – read on to find out more!

It's been a great experience meeting all the different families while filming *Save Money: Good Food*. All of them wanted to save money in the kitchen but too often there wasn't enough actual cooking from scratch going on. You don't have to be the next super star chef, you don't even have to love cooking, but if you learn the basics you'll find yourself becoming a far more flexible, and therefore economical, cook. If your recipe states 'sirloin steak' but ribeye or rump is on offer and is cheaper, with a bit of knowledge and confidence, you'll know to substitute one for the other and you'll have just saved yourself some money. Think of a recipe as an idea to build upon, rather than a hard and fast rulebook. Cooking should be fun – even relaxing – so never feel the need to stick rigidly to the ingredients list in front of you. And be a bit adventurous with your cooking – it's all very well trotting out the same old dishes every week night, but introducing new and varied foods into family meal times will generate a spark of interest and maybe even a compliment!

Wherever possible, get children involved in the preparation and cooking process. Kids are much more receptive to food if they've been involved from the start... and never underestimate them; they often surprise with their likes and dislikes. Learn to adapt your cooking styles to cater for all the family, so you're not making two or more different meals. This will save you time, money and your sanity!

Another thing to remember is that most dishes don't have to be cooked in extra virgin or expensive high-grade olive oil – cheaper olive or vegetable oil will do just fine. Save the good stuff for dressings and for finishing the dish where the flavours in the oils will really shine.

Try to be clever with food, too – by batch cooking a large meal on Monday, you'll have leftovers that can be reheated for a work lunch or even padded out and transformed into a second family meal on another night.

There are many people who'll argue that you can buy some ready meals cheaper than the cost of making them. Add to this their convenience and you can see why so many ready meals are bought in this country. Well, even if they are cheaper, they don't represent better value for money; not only will you miss out on leftovers but, as the meals are strictly portioned, you'll most likely be left feeling dissatisfied and hungry. The companies who produce these meals often replace tummy-filling, good-quality proteins and carbs with low-grade ingredients wrapped up in salt and sugar to make them taste palatable. Never believe that a ready meal is better for your health or your wallet!

In order to turn a few basic ingredients into a substantial meal or transform leftovers into something new or rejuvenate last night's extras, there are a few basic store cupboard necessities that you'll need – flour, eggs, milk, rice, pasta, caster sugar, wine vinegar, a few dried herbs and spices… All these will bring an otherwise dull dinner to life and many recipes in this book illustrate this.

Get yourself into the kitchen, arm yourself with a sharp knife and a trusty chopping board and, with a small investment of your time and energy, you'll be rewarded with good food and real money savings.

MATT TEBBUTT

INTRODUCTION

We all know we should spend less money and save more; there are infinite ways to cut down our costs, from turning off light bulbs to installing extra insulation, but this book focuses on a real hotspot of potential money saving – the kitchen. We are all guilty of overspending on food – indulging our appetites with whatever we feel like eating, instead of inventing ways of using up ingredients we already have in our fridge. A little indulgence is no bad thing, but it is the everyday wastage that hurts our pockets over time – like a little trickle of cash being constantly lost.

This book aims to help you redress that loss. With 100 recipes that can happily feed a family of four for under a fiver, you'll be able to start saving straight away. We have included some of our favourite money-saving tips, too, from how to store mushrooms to how to make soup from off cuts.

How to save money

Many of the suggestions here are not new, they've been around for a long time; you could even argue that some fall into the category of common sense. So, the first piece of advice you must heed is – stick to your guns and don't give up. It's boring but without determined self-discipline you will fail to reduce your wastage and save money and this book, along with the novelty motorised spaghetti fork and voice-activated spiraliser, may as well go to the charity shop.

Disciplined household management is a bit like going to the gym and keeping fit: it's tough at the beginning but, if you stick at it, it becomes habit and then ultimately a lifestyle. If you stay focused and self-controlled, I promise you will not only start to feel that bit richer but you will be happier, too; proud of how little waste you produce, instead of feeling guilty about how much you're chucking out.

Take stock

Before you do anything else, do a self audit. And be honest! How often do you buy ready-made or takeaway food? Do you buy ready-prepared vegetables? Ready-made sauces? Go through your receipts and add it all up – you'll be amazed how much it's costing you and, therefore, just how much you could save if you made a few small changes.

Once you've done your self audit, try a cupboard audit – what's lurking behind the oil and vinegar? How many out-of-date spices or multiple tins of beans are you hiding there? More to the point, how much food do you already have that could be turned into a meal for your family? After all, you don't want to be spending money on ingredients that you already have.

Plan, plan, plan

This is probably the single most important piece of advice you can take from this book. If you sit down for just 15 minutes at the beginning of the week, before you go off to do your shop, and construct a meal planner by thinking about which member of the family needs what meals during the week, and then make your shopping list from that, your food waste will plummet.

Of course there will be times when unforeseen circumstances, or even just your mood or appetite, affect what you want to eat. You might find yourself calling the local takeaway, instead of cooking and eating the bubble and squeak you had planned, but if you abide by your plan for the majority of the time, then you can enjoy your anomalies guilt free.

General cooking notes

★ All eggs are medium
★ All milk is semi-skimmed, unless otherwise stated
★ All stock comes from a cube, unless otherwise stated

Shopping

This is where you spend your hard-earned cash so make sure you shop smart. Almost every supermarket has a loyalty card which offers you money off in some way, shape or form; make sure you own as many as is practical. As well as loyalty cards, supermarkets offer vouchers in magazines and newspapers – use them! There's no shame in handing over a wad of coupons and watching your total tumble.

★ Slowly, slowly become an expert on supermarket prices

Pay attention to the price of products, especially the cost per kilo. You will soon find that making subtle changes will save you money; for example, pasta shapes aren't all the same price – we found penne 39p per kilo cheaper than fusilli at one major supermarket.

★ Don't be swayed by packaging

Take a look at the ingredients in a supermarket own-brand 'Basics' orange juice and compare it to the slightly more expensive own-brand variety – you may be surprised to see they are virtually the same, just dressed up differently. We found one supermarket's 'Basics' orange juice 30p per litre cheaper than their more upmarket variety. If you buy orange juice on a regular basis that money soon adds up.

★ Don't assume the supermarket is cheapest

Markets (remember them?) are open at least one day a week in most large towns and cities, and they can represent incredibly good value. Visit one and interact with the people who sell there and it'll not only be cheaper than the supermarket but it will also be a lot more fun.

★ Seek out your local ethnic store

If you are into cooking curries or other spiced foods then head down to your local ethnic store. For the price of a tiny capsule of supermarket spice you could pick up a year's worth there! Buy half that much and keep it in an airtight container in a cool, dry place. As well as being cheaper, more often than not the products are much better quality.

Learn a bit about nutrition

Learning a little about nutrition will help you make informed choices when cooking, eating and shopping. You don't need a PhD in nutrition but understanding that proteins keep your tummy full for longer and that fat-rich foods, such as nuts and eggs, are not the devil incarnate but are actually very good at keeping you fuelled for longer is a good starting point.

This is an important point for your wallet as much as for your health – often the simpler, cook-at-home options, such as porridge or scrambled eggs for breakfast, are not only cheaper to buy, but will also keep you full until lunchtime because they are nutritionally rich and will help deter you from costly snacking. Cereals or so-called breakfast bars are often really high in sugar, so they won't keep you sustained for very long.

Go vegetarian

Don't panic – I'm not suggesting you give up meat altogether and become a full-time herbivore, but your gut and bank balance will both benefit from reducing your meat intake. The easiest way to do this is to pick one day a week to go vegetarian and be strict with yourself. Meat is by far the most expensive component of any meal, so if you remove it you will find you can afford seemingly luxurious ingredients, such as Parmesan or even truffle oil.

It is also well known that large-scale production of meat can be harmful to the environment so you can sit smug in the knowledge that you are doing your bit to save the planet, too. Perhaps the greatest spin off to forcing yourself to be vegetarian once a week is that you may well find yourself becoming a better, more imaginative cook – it will take you out of your comfort zone!

Don't believe everything you read

Every product comes with a Best Before date and a Use By date but what is the difference between the two? The Use By date is the important one: it informs you of the date by which the product can be safely consumed. Take this date seriously, especially if you have a compromised immune system. If you are a hulking great adult who's in good health then you may take your chances with some bacon that has gone one day past its Use By date. I cannot advise this, but I will say that these dates err on the side of caution.

The Best Before date is very different. Any time before this date is when the manufacturer judges the product to be at its best. It means the food is still most likely fine to eat after the date – so don't throw it in the bin through paranoia.

It is important to note the difference between these two dates to avoid unnecessary wastage.

A note about costing

★ We've tried to make the recipes come in under a fiver by comparing prices at high-street supermarkets and shopping around. Obviously ingredients vary from season to season and area to area, though, so you may find dishes cost a bit more or a bit less. For the purposes of keeping the costs down, we have tended to use the supermarket budget ranges for meat, fish and other ingredients, but you may choose to do otherwise.
★ Where recipes serve more than 4, we have assumed a costing of £1.25 a head.

Look after your fridge

Avoid cluttering up your fridge – fresh food needs air circulating around it to keep it cool. The more crowded your fridge is, the hotter it will get and the quicker your food will spoil. And clean your fridge regularly – you don't want mould growing, which can make other foods go off.

A few fridge tips:

★ **Fresh fruit** You can make strawberries and raspberries last longer by washing them in a vinegar and water mix before putting them in the fridge – this kills the mould spores. One part white vinegar to ten parts water means it'll be diluted enough not to affect the flavour.

If you get home from the supermarket and notice a mouldy berry in your punnet, remove it straight away, as it can cause others to start going bad.

Only using half an avocado? Brush the unused half with olive oil or lemon juice to stop it browning. Also, you could keep the stone in the half of the avocado you don't use, which will also prevent it from going brown as quickly.

★ **Dairy products** Avoid storing milk in the fridge door – it is the place in the fridge where the temperature fluctuates the most, which can cause milk to spoil more quickly. For this same reason, though, it's a good idea to store mayonnaise there – it may get too cold in the inner part of the fridge, which will cause it to separate.

Store ricotta or cottage cheese upside down in the fridge to keep it fresh longer – this creates a vacuum, stopping bacteria from growing.

Harness the power of your freezer

Your freezer is a great asset. Used properly it is a treasure chest of homely food just waiting to be defrosted and reheated. Used wrongly and it is a graveyard of icy food that will give you an upset tummy. If you've neglected your freezer then give it a clean start by defrosting it, going through all the contents and throwing out anything you aren't really going to eat.

The key to good freezer management is organisation, sticky labels and stock rotation. Stick a label on whatever you decide to freeze with a brief description and the date it entered the freezer. This means you can avoid food lurking in the shadows for years and turning into useless, energy-guzzling lumps of waste.

Any fresh food, such as meat, that goes into the freezer should be frozen when it is as fresh as possible. Any cooked food for the freezer should be cooled to at least room temperature before being tightly wrapped and labelled.

Be sure to think practically about portion sizes when freezing. There is no point freezing a huge 2-litre block of chicken stock – use vessels, such as plastic drinks cups, to portion out amounts; that way, when you come to use it, you can defrost only what you need.

You can freeze more foods than you might think. Here are some that you might not have realised can be frozen:

★ **Fresh fruit** Almost any fruit can be frozen. For best results be sure to lay the fruit in a single layer over a flat baking sheet lined with parchment before freezing. Then, when frozen, transfer the fruit to sealable bags. Frozen fruit can be put straight into the blender for smoothies or even cooked from frozen in a crumble. Freeze any leftover juices or smoothies to make ice lollies.

★ **Dairy products** These freeze very well. If you ever find you have a glut of butter then be sure to freeze it. If you're into making pastry then often butter straight from the freezer will give better results than that at room temperature – just be sure to freeze it in weighed amounts. Milk is another dairy product that can be frozen – just be sure to pour out a small glassful before freezing to avoid a burst bottle. Keeping ice cream in a Ziploc plastic bag in the freezer will keep it soft enough to scoop every time.

★ **Eggs** If a recipe only calls for the yolks then be sure to put the whites into a sealable bag and freeze them. Once defrosted, they whip up into a perfect meringue. Yolks don't freeze very well so just add them to your normal scrambled eggs for a touch of extra luxury.

★ **Lemon and lime juice** These may seem like obvious ingredients to freeze, but have you thought of putting them in ice cube trays? If you do, they are perfect for your Friday night gin and tonic, or adding to a sauce to give it a hint of fresh tartness just before serving.

★ **Bread** Don't just freeze the whole loaf or batch of rolls – if you have bread that is growing old then blitz it up into crumbs and freeze in a sealable bag. Freeze sliced bread at the beginning of the week after your weekly shop and then just toast as needed – give it a little bang before freezing to avoid the slices sticking together as much. You can make sandwiches with frozen bread – make them in the morning and they will defrost by lunchtime, and will help to keep your filling cool. If you find yourself throwing out the crusty ends of a loaf of bread, try turning them into garlic bread instead. Give bread that's going a little stale a 10 second microwave blast to freshen it up.

★ **Pasta** Leftover pasta can be rinsed in cold water and then frozen, ready to be reheated in the microwave.

★ **Herbs** So often you buy a large packet of herbs for a particular recipe, use a little bit of them and then the rest just slowly turn to mush in the back of the fridge. Next time, roughly chop up the leftover herbs, stalk and all, and freeze in a sealable bag. The herbs can be used from frozen to finish off stews, risottos and sauces. Use a microwave to dry leftover fresh herbs (thick-leaved herbs like rosemary, thyme and oregano are best) – pick the leaves off and spread them on a plate covered with kitchen roll. Cover them with another sheet of kitchen roll and microwave for a minute, followed by short bursts until they're completely dry – they should be starting to crumble when handled. Store them whole or use a pestle and mortar to grind them first; they'll last for several months this way.

★ **Fresh vegetables** Just like when you freeze fresh fruit, be sure to prepare the vegetables first – so separate out broccoli florets and spread chopped onions flat in a single layer on a flat baking tray lined with parchment – and, when frozen, pile them into a sealable bag. Frozen veg can be a great lower cost alternative to buying fresh and, as you just need to open the bag and take out the amount you actually need to use each time, you won't run the risk of buying the same quantity of fresh produce and it going off.

Stop wasting fruit, vegetables and herbs that are going a little limp and past their best. You can do the following and keep them in the freezer to live again another time.

★ **Make pesto** Whiz up soft, fresh herbs that might be past their best with enough vegetable or light olive oil to create a smooth consistency and then pour the pesto into ice cube trays and freeze. The herb oil can then be added frozen to pasta sauces and risottos – it'll melt in and add extra flavour.

★ **Make tasty vegetable sauce** Sweat down an onion in oil then add in almost any vegetable from cauliflower to broccoli stalks, fry for a few more minutes then add tinned tomatoes and vegetable stock. Bring the whole lot to the boil and then, when all the ingredients are tender, blitz until smooth. Portion up the sauce and use it as an instant sauce that you know is filled with vegetable goodness.

Keep a well-stocked store cupboard

Your store cupboard should become a reliable and well-used treasure trove of ingredients from which you can whip up a quick meal. The following is a list of what we would consider essentials:

★ **Tomato puree** can be so much more than a nonchalant ingredient added to bolognaise. Be sure to 'cook out' the puree. This means frying it in amongst all the other ingredients for 1 minute before adding any liquid. It deepens the flavour.

★ **Light soy sauce** brings an instant salty depth to almost any dish. Don't limit its use to Asian meals – a little splash in a rich beef stew will bring a new dimension to an old classic. Opt for light soy sauce instead of dark – it gives you more bang for your buck in terms of flavour.

★ **Stock cubes** are the lifeblood of your cupboard. Their use knows no bounds. Be sure always to have chicken stock cubes on hand (unless of course you are vegetarian) as they are by far the most versatile. They're so cheap and last forever so you may as well have beef and vegetable stock cubes on standby, too.

★ **Plain flour** is the king of your pantry. From thickening stews to making cakes and bread, you will definitely need flour. Plain flour is the most versatile of them all and is also the cheapest, so aim to have a bag always to hand.

★ **Spices** add flavour to every meal, especially those dishes you've been cooking for years and are sick at the thought of. Don't go overboard, though, as they can be expensive and will go stale after a while. I'd recommend having garam masala, ground coriander, smoked paprika and chilli powder as a starting point.

★ **Rice** is an obvious contender for the store cupboard because it's cheap and doesn't go off. Don't assume that all rice grains are good for all dishes – I recommend storing basmati rice as your all-rounder and arborio for risottos.

★ **Pasta** is already in most people's cupboard. It is one of the easiest, most filling ingredients available to you. Even when it is simply boiled, seasoned with salt and pepper and a little cheese, pasta is both comforting and delicious.

A few store cupboard tips:

★ Rub a small amount of vegetable oil around the top of a screw top jar to avoid it getting sticky and crusty.

★ Store honey in the cupboard and not the fridge or it will crystallise.

★ If you've got some baking powder and you don't know if it has gone past its expiry date, don't just throw it out – add half a teaspoon of it to boiling water – if it quickly bubbles a lot, it's still good. If there's only a little fizzing or none at all, it's time to throw it out.

It is easy to make your own flavoured oils, which can be used to add a punch to your dishes. Making garlic, chilli or herb oils is also a great way to use up extra fresh ingredients:

★ To make herby garlic oil

Stuff about 6 sprigs each of rosemary and thyme into a clean glass bottle or jar, add 8 peeled garlic cloves and pour in a litre of light olive oil or vegetable oil. Leave in a cool, dark place to infuse for a week and then use – the taste will grow stronger the longer the oil is left to steep.

★ To make chilli oil

Prick 6–10 chillies (depending on how hot you like things) all over with a knife and then stuff them into a clean glass bottle or jar. Pour over about a litre of light olive oil or vegetable oil and leave to steep for a week before using.

SPEEDY
SUPPERS

MEGA MUSHROOMS ON TOAST

 SERVES 4

As soon as you cut meat out of a recipe you find yourself flush with cash to spend on things like good bread or good cheese. In this recipe we swap the meat for sourdough and blue cheese. Don't be tempted to peel your mushrooms, so much of the flavour and nutritional value is guarded within the skin. Simply brush them clean with a dry tea towel.

PREP TIME 10 MINUTES
COOKING TIME 15 MINUTES

1 tbsp butter

1 tbsp olive oil

1 clove garlic, peeled and
   finely chopped

800g chestnut mushrooms,
   brushed clean and roughly
   cut into ½cm slices

2 sprigs of thyme

4 eggs

4 thick slices of sourdough
   bread

75ml double cream

50g blue cheese
   (such as Gorgonzola)

1 small handful of fresh chives,
   finely sliced

Put a large pot of water on to boil for poaching the eggs later.

Heat the butter and oil together in a large frying pan over a medium to high heat. When hot, add the garlic and fry for 30 seconds. Cram in the mushrooms and sprinkle in the thyme. Fry, turning regularly, for about 4 minutes, or until the mushrooms have browned in a few spots and have softened.

Crack the eggs into the large pot of boiling water and reduce the heat right down so the water is barely bubbling. Cook the eggs like this for 4–5 minutes for a soft yolk. Meanwhile, put the bread on to toast.

Reduce the heat under the mushrooms to medium and pour in the cream. Bring the cream up to a gentle simmer and then stir in the cheese until it has melted into the sauce. If you feel the sauce is becoming too thick, then pour in a little water to loosen.

Serve the mushrooms on the toast, topped with a poached egg and a sprinkling of chives.

TIP

Store mushrooms in a paper bag, rather than a plastic one, to make them last longer

PANZANELLA

SERVES 4

This is a great way of using up slightly old bread and makes for a perfect side dish to a grilled peice of fish or meat. Anchovies are a traditional way of bringing flavour to dishes and they are so cheap. Just don't tell anyone they're in there and then they can't be squeamish about them.

PREP TIME 10 MINUTES
COOKING TIME 15 MINUTES

—

4 thick slices of bread
(roughly 200g)
4 slices of serrano ham, each
roughly cut into 3 pieces
300g very ripe tomatoes, roughly
chopped into 3cm chunks
1 tbsp olive oil
½ red onion, peeled and very
finely diced
1 small bunch of fresh basil,
roughly torn, stalks and leaves
4 anchovy fillets (roughly 12g)
1 tbsp capers

Preheat the oven to 100°C/Gas ¼.

Roughly tear up the bread into big chunks then put on a baking tray and slide into the preheated oven. Cook for about 5 minutes.

Add the ham to the tray and cook with the bread for a further 8–10 minutes, or until the bread has dried out a little and gone a bit crusty.

Place the tomatoes in a bowl and add the olive oil, onion and most of the basil, along with a good pinch of pepper.

Drain about half of the oil from the anchovy tin into the bowl and then chop up the anchovy fillets into very small pieces and add to the bowl, too.

Toss all the salad ingredients together and then add the bread, toss again and serve immediately with a little scattering of leftover basil.

TUNA & TOMATO GRILLED CHEESE SANDWICH

SERVES 2

The grilled cheese sandwich is a thing of unrivalled ugly beauty, a wonderful concoction that the sophisticated amongst us would love to hate, but it just tastes so darned good! Be sure to keep the drained liquid from the tinned tomatoes; it would make the sandwich too soggy but can be used in other dishes from bolognaise to soup.

PREP TIME 10 MINUTES
COOKING TIME 10 MINUTES

100g baby spinach
1 x 400g tin chopped tomatoes
1 x 160g tin tuna, drained
½ red onion, peeled and
    finely diced
75g mozzarella, grated (pizza-
    style hard mozzarella is best)
2 tbsp butter
4 thick slices of bread
salad, to serve

Put a kettle of water on to boil. Tip the spinach into a colander and pour the boiling water over the top to wilt it. When nicely wilted, run cold water over the leaves until they are cool enough to handle.

Pick up the wilted spinach and squeeze hard in your hands to remove as much excess liquid as possible. Roughly chop and drop into a bowl.

Tip the tomatoes into a sieve over another bowl and leave to drain almost all of the liquid. Tip the drained tomato into the bowl with the spinach.

Flake in the tuna, breaking it up into chunks with a fork as you add it to the mix.

Mix in the onion and mozzarella, along with a good pinch of both salt and pepper.

Butter the slices of bread and put a griddle pan, or heavy-based, non-stick frying pan over a medium to high heat. When hot, lay two pieces of bread in the pan, butter side down.

Pile the mixture equally between the two slices of bread and then lay the remaining buttered slices of bread on top, butter side up, and push down a little. Fry the sandwiches for 2 minutes and then carefully flip and cook for a further 2 minutes.

The filling should be warmed through and the cheese perfectly melted. Serve with a little salad.

TIP

Don't like crusts on your sandwiches? Once you've cut them off, keep them in the freezer and, when you have enough, use them to make breadcrumbs.

SHAKSHOUKA
& FLATBREADS

SERVES **4**

Every cookbook in the last year seems to have a recipe for shakshouka in it and so here's our addition to the shakshouka recipe library. To give you a little more bang for your buck, we've thrown in a flatbread recipe, too.

PREP TIME 20 MINUTES
COOKING TIME 30 MINUTES

40ml olive oil
2 red onions, peeled and sliced
2 red peppers, de-seeded
   and diced
100g chorizo, peeled and
   cut into 1cm cubes
1 tsp ground cumin
1 tbsp tomato puree
2 x 400g tins chopped tomatoes
250g self-raising flour, plus
   a little extra for dusting
8 eggs
1 small bunch of fresh parsley,
   roughly chopped

Heat half the oil in a large, high-sided frying pan over a medium heat. When hot, add the onions, red pepper and chorizo and gently fry for about 8 minutes, or until the vegetables are softening and the chorizo is releasing its red oil.

Turn up the heat a little and add the cumin and tomato puree and continue to fry, stirring regularly, for 2 minutes.

Stir in the tomatoes. Half fill one of the empty tins with water and add this, too. Bring the mixture up to the boil and simmer for 10 minutes, or until the sauce has thickened a little and the vegetables are nice and tender.

Whilst the shakshouka is simmering away, make the flatbreads by mixing together the flour, about 125ml of water and a good pinch of salt, until you reach a soft dough. Knead for 2 minutes and then divide the mix into 6 smallish balls. Dust a surface with flour and roll out each ball until it is about ¾ cm thick. Don't worry about the shape, concentrate on reaching an even thickness.

When all the balls are rolled out, heat a griddle pan or heavy-based frying pan over a high heat and lightly brush the breads with a little of the remaining oil. When the pan is hot, dry fry the flatbreads for 2 minutes on each side. Remove to a plate and keep warm.

When the shakshouka has had its 10 minutes, use a spoon to prod 8 hollows into the mix and crack an egg into each one. Place a lid quickly on top (use a baking tray or large plate if you don't have a lid) and cook for 4 minutes.

Just before serving with the flatbreads, season the shakshouka with salt and pepper and scatter with the parsley.

PRAWN SPAGHETTI WITH PUTTANESCA SAUCE

SERVES 4

Tomatoes that are going soft are perfect for a quick sauce. If you have any Shakshouka left over (page 31), you can use the sauce here instead of making one from scratch (this is what we've done for the photo) – just add the anchovies and chilli flakes from the ingredients list below to give it a puttanesca kick.

PREP TIME 10 MINUTES
COOKING TIME 15 MINUTES

___

350g wholemeal spaghetti
200g cooked and frozen
    prawns, defrosted
1 tbsp olive oil
3 anchovy fillets (about 10g),
    drained and finely chopped
1 tsp chilli flakes
2–3 small shallots, peeled and
    finely chopped
1 large sprig of rosemary
1 clove garlic, peeled and
    finely chopped
100g very ripe tomatoes,
    roughly chopped into
    large chunks

Bring a large pan of water to the boil and, when boiling, drop in the spaghetti and cook according to packet instructions. Three minutes before the spaghetti is due to be ready, add the prawns.

While the spaghetti is cooking, heat the oil in a saucepan over a low heat and add the anchovies, chilli, shallots, rosemary and garlic. Cook for 8 minutes, or until the shallots are just starting to soften.

Crank up the heat to medium high, add the tomatoes and cook for a further 5 minutes, or until the tomatoes have just started to collapse. Increase the heat again and let the sauce bubble for 3 minutes.

Just before draining the cooked pasta and prawns, hive off half a mugful of cooking liquid and keep to one side.

Drain the spaghetti and prawns and toss them into the pot with the sauce. Turn the heat up to maximum and pour in half of the saved cooking liquid.

Toss all the ingredients together until they are well coated, adding more cooking liquid if you need it.

Serve straight away.

TIP

*Keep the oil drained from anchovies –
it's bursting with flavour – and use it to dress
salads or even to enhance plain pasta.*

SMOKED HADDOCK & SPINACH OMELETTE

SERVES 4

A classic flavour combination inspired by the omelette Arnold Bennett. Smoked haddock is a flavourful and economic way to eat fish; available at almost any supermarket, you should always have a chunk of it in your fridge. This is the perfect meal for a busy household when you have many mouths to feed but not all at the same time – make the filling in advance and you're only ever 3 minutes away from satisfying a hungry family member.

PREP TIME 15 MINUTES
COOKING TIME 30 MINUTES

—

500ml milk
1 bay leaf
outer layers of 1 onion (30g)
250g smoked haddock
100g spinach
75g butter
60g plain flour
100g cooked prawns (little ones)
grating of nutmeg
12 eggs

Pour the milk into a saucepan, add the bay leaf and onion and bring to the boil. When boiling, slide the haddock into the pan, return to the boil, cover with a lid and remove the pan from the heat. Leave to sit for 10 minutes, by which time the haddock will be cooked and the milk infused with the smoky flavour.

Bring a kettle to the boil and drop the spinach into a colander. Pour boiling water over the spinach, which will wilt with the heat. Use a spoon to move the spinach about in the residual steam and then leave to cool.

Carefully remove the haddock from the milk and put to one side. Strain the bay leaf and onion from the milk.

Heat 35g of the butter in a clean pan over a medium heat. When melted and bubbling, sprinkle in the flour and stir together. Fry, stirring continuously, for 2 minutes, then add a ladleful of the milk, stirring to avoid lumps. When the first ladleful has been absorbed, add a second. Repeat this process until you have a thick, smooth sauce. Turn off the heat.

Peel the skin from the haddock and break the flesh into the sauce. The spinach should be cool enough to handle so give it a good squeeze to remove as much liquid as possible. Roughly chop the spinach and add to the sauce, along with the prawns, nutmeg and a good pinch of both salt and pepper. The filling is now ready.

To make an omelette, crack 3 eggs into a bowl and whisk gently. Heat 10g of the butter in a small (15cm) non-stick frying pan over a medium to high heat. When melted and bubbling, pour in the egg. Draw in the egg from the edges of the pan, until the majority is cooked through. Spoon a quarter of the filling on to one side of the omelette and then flip the second side over.

Repeat with the rest of the eggs to make 4 omelettes.

CRAB STICK FU YUNG

SERVES 4

The crab stick is much-maligned – its hyper-pink appearance and weird packaging make for a pretty uncomfortable ingredient. But there is a reason why they are still on the supermarket shelves – they are delicious and are a good, cheap source of fish. They're not made from crab, instead they are a mixture of different fish – think of them as an aquatic sausage and suddenly they become more desirable.

PREP TIME 15 MINUTES, PLUS
15 MINUTES SOAKING TIME
COOKING TIME 25 MINUTES
———

250g jasmine rice
8 eggs
2 tbsp light soy sauce
1 tbsp sesame oil
1 tbsp sunflower oil
40g shiitake mushrooms, brushed clean and cut thinly
5 spring onions, white and green separated, both sliced
1 red chilli, de-seeded and finely sliced
1 green chilli, de-seeded and finely sliced
200g seafood sticks, unwrapped and cut in half
75g baby spinach

Tip the rice into a large bowl, cover with water and leave to soak for 15 minutes.

Drain the rice and tip into a saucepan. Pour over 250ml of water, which should just poke up over the rice and bring the water to the boil over a high heat. Cover and reduce the heat to minimum. Leave the rice to cook like this for 12 minutes – DO NOT peek and DO NOT stir. After 12 minutes turn the heat off completely and leave to sit for a further 5 minutes – only then can you peek and fluff up the perfect rice with a fork.

Whilst the rice is cooking, crack the eggs into a large bowl and beat in both the soy sauce and sesame oil.

Heat the sunflower oil in a large, non-stick frying pan over a high heat and, when hot, add the mushrooms, the white part of the spring onions and both the red and green chillies (leave a little chilli behind for garnish). Stir-fry the ingredients together for 2 minutes, then add the seafood sticks and spinach and continue to stir-fry for a further 2 minutes.

Pour the egg into the pan and, a bit like when you cook an omelette, wait for the egg to set around the edges of the pan and then draw the cooked parts into the centre, refilling the gap they leave with uncooked egg. Continue the process until the majority of egg is cooked and then leave the egg to brown for 1 minute, before finally taking it off the heat.

Slice the fu yung into large chunks and serve on top of some rice, sprinkled with the reserved chilli and the spring onion greens.

TIP

Although it doesn't need to be chilled, putting soy sauce in the fridge will help retain its flavour.

SMOKED MACKEREL TAGLIATELLE

SERVES 4

Smoked mackerel is a gift to those on a budget. On top of its deliciously smoky flavour, it is incredibly good for you, packed with those omega 3 fats that everybody lectures you about eating. You could make this even quicker by using fresh pasta – that would take the cooking time of this recipe down to about 5 mintues!

PREP TIME 5 MINUTES
COOKING TIME 15 MINUTES

——

350g tagliatelle
1 tbsp olive oil
2 shallots, peeled
   and finely chopped
1 clove garlic, peeled
   and finely chopped
125g mascarpone
½ lemon, juice only
225g smoked mackerel, skin
   removed and flesh broken
   into large chunks
½ small bunch of fresh
   parsley, finely chopped

Bring a large pot of water to the boil and cook the pasta according to packet instructions. Just before draining, scoop out a quarter of a mugful of the cooking liquid and keep to one side.

Whilst the pasta is cooking, heat the oil in a large frying pan over a medium heat and, when hot, add the shallots and garlic. Cook, stirring regularly, for about 4 minutes, or until the ingredients have softened.

Add the marscapone, the reserved cooking liquid and season well with pepper. Bring to a simmer and then squeeze in the lemon juice. Turn off the heat and gently stir through the smoked mackerel and parsley.

Tip the drained pasta into the pan with the other ingredients and lightly toss the pasta in the sauce to coat.

Serve straight away.

COD FILLETS WITH GARLIC BUTTER & CAULIFLOWER RICE

SERVES 2

Cod is a great fish to give people who don't think they like fish – it has a good, large flake to it and a very neutral flavour. It's bound to win them over! Cauliflower rice has become fashionable recently with those who don't like to eat carbs, but here we're choosing it for its flavour.

PREP TIME 15 MINUTES
COOKING TIME 15 MINUTES

———

80g butter, softened
2 cloves garlic, peeled and
    finely minced
½ small bunch of fresh chives,
    finely chopped
½ small bunch of fresh parsley,
    finely chopped
½ large cauliflower, green
    leaves and stalk removed
2 tbsp vegetable oil
1 tsp ground cumin
1 tsp smoked paprika
2 spring onions, trimmed
    and finely sliced
2 x 175g cod fillets, skin off
2 tbsp plain flour
50g rocket, to serve

Place the softened butter in a bowl and add the garlic, chives and parsley, as well as a good pinch of both salt and pepper. Beat the ingredients together until you have a smooth mix. Dollop the butter on to a piece of clingfilm, then roll up into a sausage shape and leave in the fridge to cool.

Blitz the cauliflower in a food processor until the florets have broken down to resemble rough couscous or rice.

Heat half the oil in a large frying pan over a high heat. When hot, add the cauliflower and stir-fry for 5 minutes, or until it is tender.

Turn the heat right down, add the spices and spring onions, along with a good pinch of salt and pepper, and toss everything together. Turn off the heat and keep to one side.

Heat the remaining oil in a large, non-stick frying pan. Lightly dust the cod all over with the flour and a good pinch of both salt and pepper. When the oil is hot, add the cod to the pan and fry for about 3 minutes on each side. Turn the heat down to medium and add the flavoured butter.

Continue to cook the cod, turning regularly in the flavoured butter, for a further 5 minutes, or until the fish is cooked through.

Serve the cauliflower rice topped with a piece of cod and a small handful of rocket on the side.

SMOKY CHICKEN QUESADILLA

SERVES 4

It doesn't seem fair to label quesadillas as just another repackaging of leftover foods because they can be so much more. A quesadilla is basically a grilled cheese sandwich made using tortillas instead of bread – what you jam inside the tortillas is up to you. In this recipe we've gone for a Mexican-inspired smoky chicken and cheese combination.

PREP TIME 10 MINUTES
COOKING TIME 20 MINUTES

1½ tbsp vegetable oil
½ small bunch of fresh
   coriander, leaves and stalks
   separated and both chopped
1 red onion, peeled and diced
1 red pepper, de-seeded
   and sliced
2 cloves garlic, peeled
   and finely chopped
200g chicken breast,
   cut into thin slices
2 tsp tomato puree
1 tsp smoked paprika
1 tsp ground cumin
1 x 400g tin black-eyed beans,
   drained and rinsed
150ml chicken stock
2 large flour tortillas
50g Cheddar, grated

Heat the oil in a large frying pan over a medium heat and, when hot, add the coriander stalks, onion, red pepper and garlic and fry for 4 minutes, or until the onion has softened.

Turn up the heat to maximum and add the chicken. Fry everything together for 2 minutes – you're not trying to cook the chicken through, just colour it a little.

Add the tomato puree and spices and continue to fry for another minute.

Finally, add the beans and stock. Bring the liquid up to a simmer and cook, uncovered, for 10 minutes, or until the beans are soft and have absorbed much of the stock.

Turn off the heat, stir in the coriander leaves, keeping a few to one side as a garnish, and then tip the mix into a bowl and leave to cool a little.

Clean out the frying pan and place over a medium heat.

Lay a tortilla on the base of the frying pan and spoon the chicken mixture on top, spreading it out to cover the tortilla evenly. Sprinkle over the cheese and then place the second tortilla on top.

Cook for about 3 minutes and then lay a large plate or chopping board on top of the frying pan. Place one hand on top and flip the pan over, releasing the quesadilla. Put the pan back on the heat, slide in the quesadilla on the uncooked side and fry for a final 3 minutes.

Cut into 4 thick wedges and serve, sprinkled with the reserved coriander leaves.

BACON TORTILLA

SERVES 4

In this sort of dish a little goes a long way so you only need a small amount of bacon to flavour a big tortilla. Eggs are the perfect food; filled with protein and fat, they'll keep you fuelled all day. This is great the next day served at room temperature for lunch.

PREP TIME 10 MINUTES
COOKING TIME 20 MINUTES

—

250g potatoes, peeled and
    cut into 3cm chunks
2 tbsp vegetable oil
6 rashers smoked streaky bacon,
    cut into 1cm thick slices
1 onion, peeled and finely sliced
1 red pepper, de-seeded and
    finely sliced
12 eggs
40g Cheddar, grated
1 tbsp olive oil
2 tsp Dijon mustard
40ml white wine vinegar
100g mixed salad, to serve

Bring a large pot of water to the boil and simmer the potatoes for about 12 minutes, or until they are just cooked through and tender. Drain through a colander and leave to steam to get them as dry as possible.

Whilst the potatoes are cooking, heat the vegetable oil in a 18cm non-stick frying pan over a low heat. When hot, add the bacon, onion and red pepper, and cook gently for 12 minutes, or until the vegetables are soft and the bacon lightly browned.

Crack the eggs into a bowl and give them a good whisk, before adding a pinch of salt and pepper.

Preheat the grill to maximum.

Increase the heat under the pan to maximum and, when hot, drop in the potatoes and toss with the other ingredients – they will break up, but don't worry too much. Try and brown a few potatoes.

Turn the heat down to medium and pour in the beaten egg. As it cooks, drag the cooked egg at the outside edges of the pan into the middle to let raw egg flow into the void left behind. Repeat this process until the mixture in the pan resembles scrambled egg.

Now fry the tortilla for 1 minute, without turning or moving, and then sprinkle the top with the cheese.

Slide under the hot grill and cook for 1–2 minutes, or until the top of the tortilla is golden and browned.

Remove from the grill and leave to sit for 2 minutes.

Whisk together the olive oil, mustard and vinegar until you reach a smooth emulsion.

Serve wedges of tortilla with the salad and dressing on the side.

LAKSA

This is easier to make than you might presume. This sort of dish is brilliant because you can use almost any ingredients in it. Make the most of your coconut milk by separating the solids (the cream) from the milk. The milk will always be good for smoothies and the cream can be diluted into curries and soups like this. Everybody thinks pork belly has to be cooked for hours on end, but it can also be cooked quickly under the grill.

PREP TIME 25 MINUTES,
PLUS 1 HOUR MARINATING
COOKING TIME 30 MINUTES

—

2 cloves garlic, peeled and minced
4cm ginger, peeled and minced
2½ tbsp light soy sauce
300g pork belly, cut into strips
300g dried noodles (from super
   noodles to egg noodles)
1 tbsp vegetable oil
1 lime, zest and juice
1½ tsp rose harissa
   (or ½ tsp chilli flakes)
30g lemongrass, finely chopped
3 anchovy fillets (about 10g),
   finely chopped, plus
   1 tbsp of the oil
200g coconut milk solids
   (the cream)
750ml chicken stock
50g baby spinach
100g beansprouts

Place half the garlic, half the ginger and half the soy sauce into a bowl and add the pork. Work the ingredients into the meat and leave to marinate for at least one hour.

When you're ready to eat, bring a pan of water to the boil and cook the noodles according to the packet instructions. Drain through a colander and rinse under cold water to cool.

Turn the grill to maximum and line the grill tray with a piece of tin foil or baking parchment.

Heat the vegetable oil in a large wok or saucepan over a high heat. When hot, add the remaining garlic and ginger and stir-fry for 30 seconds before adding the lime zest, harissa, lemongrass and anchovies with their oil and fry for 2 minutes.

Pour in the coconut cream and stock, bring the liquid to the boil and simmer for 5 minutes.

Meanwhile, lay the pork on the lined grill tray. Cook for 6–7 minutes on each side, or until you are happy the pork is cooked through and lightly charred in places.

Divide the cooked noodles between 4 bowls, pour over the boiling soup and top with the spinach and beansprouts. Cut the pork belly strips into smaller pieces and finish the Laksa by placing the pork on top.

TURKEY JAMBALAYA

SERVES 6

Bacon packs so much flavour per gram, so it's a great way of flavouring big carbs, such as the rice in this recipe.

PREP TIME 15 MINUTES
COOKING TIME 25 MINUTES

1½ tbsp vegetable oil
100g chorizo, cut into 1cm pieces
2 onions, peeled and diced
2 green peppers, de-seeded and diced
2 celery stalks, washed and diced, leaves kept and roughly chopped
300g turkey breast, cut into 1cm strips
1 tbsp dried oregano
2 tsp dried thyme
2 tsp sweet paprika
250g long grain rice
1 x 400g tin chopped tomatoes
300ml chicken stock

Heat the oil in a large, high-sided frying pan over a medium to high heat. When hot, add the chorizo, onions, green peppers and celery and stir-fry for 5 minutes.

Turn up the heat to maximum and add the turkey. Continue to stir-fry everything for a further 2 minutes, by which time the turkey should have taken on a little colour. Sprinkle in the oregano, thyme and paprika and stir into the other ingredients.

Tip in the rice, tomatoes and stock, along with a good pinch of both salt and pepper. Bring the liquid up to a simmer, cover with a lid (use a big plate if you don't have a lid) and cook, covered, for 15 minutes.

Turn off the heat and leave to sit for 5 minutes.

When ready to eat, remove the lid, rough up the rice with a fork and sprinkle with the celery leaves before serving.

TIP

Don't presume your spices will last forever! They do go off, so be sure to try and use the whole tub before buying more.

BAKED EGGS WITH SAUSAGES & KALE

SERVES 4

Baked eggs have somewhat disappeared into the annals of culinary history – but it's time for them to break out. By baking them in the oven, you can cater for a crowd without the pressure of having to cook individual eggs to order. Eggs are the original superfood, brimming with nutrients to keep you going and, just as important, they are cheap and accessible, too.

PREP TIME 10 MINUTES
COOKING TIME 30 MINUTES

———

1 tbsp vegetable oil
8 sausages
2 dried chillies
125g mushrooms, brushed clean
    and chopped into quarters
200g kale, chopped
6 eggs
50g breadcrumbs
8 sage leaves, chopped
40g Cheddar, grated
4 thick slices of bread,
    to serve

Preheat the oven to 200°C/Gas 6.

Heat the oil in an ovenproof frying pan over a medium heat. When hot, add the sausages and fry for 8 minutes, turning a few times in the hot oil to brown all over. The sausages don't have to be fully cooked at this point.

Add the chillies and mushrooms and fry, stirring regularly, for 2 minutes.

Drop in the kale and continue to fry for a further 5 minutes, or until the kale has wilted and is tender.

Turn the heat right down to low and use a wooden spoon to make 6 indentations. Crack an egg into each little one.

Mix together the breadcrumbs and sage and sprinkle all over the top of the dish, along with the cheese and a good grinding of pepper.

Slide the pan into the preheated oven and bake for 5 minutes.

Whilst the eggs are cooking, toast the slices of bread.

Serve generous helpings of egg, kale and sausage on top of the toasted bread, or alternatively eat straight out of the pan.

TIP

Don't throw away herbs. Fresh herbs such as sage and rosemary freeze brilliantly or, alternatively, dry them out in your airing cupboard and keep them in an airtight container.

CHORIZO & SPINACH FRITTATA

SERVES 4

Potatoes, onions and deliciously spicy chorizo all wrapped up in a wonderful omelette finished with melted cheese – what's not to like? Frittatas are a brilliant way of feeding your family quickly and cheaply – onions, eggs and potatoes are always the base, but you can throw almost any vegetable or meat into the mix and end up with a very satisfying meal.

PREP TIME 10 MINUTES
COOKING TIME 25 MINUTES

175g potatoes, scrubbed clean
   and cut into 3cm chunks
1½ tbsp vegetable oil
1 onion, peeled and finely sliced
65g chorizo, cut into 1cm cubes
12 eggs
100g baby spinach, plus
   extra to serve
70g Cheddar, grated

Preheat the grill to high.

Bring a pot of water to the boil and cook the potatoes for about 10 minutes, or until they are very tender. Drain them through a colander and give them a good shake to remove as much of the excess liquid as possible.

Whilst the potatoes are boiling, heat the oil in a large, non-stick frying pan over a medium heat. Slide in the onion and chorizo, and cook together for 8–10 minutes, or until the onion is meltingly soft and lightly coloured.

Crack the eggs into a bowl, season with a little pepper and whisk together.

Crank up the heat under the onion and chorizo to maximum and carefully add the potatoes. Fry together for about 2 minutes – it's nice to get a little colour on the potatoes, if possible. Pile in the spinach and carefully turn in the pan to wilt.

Pour the beaten eggs into the pan and, still over the high heat, begin to draw the cooked edges in from the edges of the pan. Cook for about 3–4 minutes, or until almost all of the egg is cooked through – it will still be a little wobbly on top, but don't worry.

Sprinkle the cheese all over the surface of the frittata and slide the pan under the preheated grill (if your pan has a plastic handle, be sure to leave it poking out or it will melt). Grill for 3–4 minutes, or until the top is bubbling and golden.

Carefully slide the frittata from the pan, cut into large wedges and serve with a handful of baby spinach leaves.

TWICE-COOKED LOADED SKINS

SERVES 4

The skin of a potato is not only the most nutritionally dense part, but it is arguably the tastiest. Combine the skin with a cheesy, bacon-flavoured filling and this recipe will be one you pull out once a week. If you don't have a microwave then bake the potatoes in the oven as you would normally – less speedy but equally delicious.

PREP TIME 10 MINUTES
COOKING TIME 25 MINUTES

4 large potatoes
1 tbsp vegetable oil
1 tbsp butter
3 rashers smoked streaky bacon, cut into 1cm strips
1 onion, peeled and diced
1 sprig of thyme, leaves only
25g cream cheese
50g Cheddar, grated
salad, to serve

Preheat the oven to 180°C/Gas 4.

Scrub the potatoes clean and then pat them dry and brush all over with the oil. Prick with a fork and zap in the microwave for 4 minutes. Leave to rest for 2 minutes and then zap them again for a further 4 minutes. Repeat the process until the potatoes are cooked through on the inside. Leave to cool a little.

Whilst the potatoes are cooking, heat the butter in a large frying pan over a medium to high heat and, when melted and bubbling, add the bacon, onion and thyme and fry for 5 minutes, or until the bacon is cooked through and the onion is soft. Leave to cool a little.

When the potatoes are cool enough to handle, cut them open and scoop the soft flesh into a bowl, being careful not to penetrate the potato skin.

Scrape the bacon mixture into the cooked potato flesh and add the cream cheese, along with a good grind of both salt and pepper. Beat together until well mixed.

Spoon the mixture back into the potato halves – you will have to pack them tight and pile them high. Scatter the Cheddar over the top and bake in the oven for about 15 minutes, or until the cheese is golden and bubbling.

Serve with a small side salad.

TIP

Stale or hard cheese can be grated into mash or used in pasta and chilli dishes.

KOREAN PORK RICE BOWL

SERVES 4

This is your basic bowl of hot, steaming yumminess that you would gladly pay more than a fiver for. At its base is seasoned rice, which acts as the perfect wingman to the savouriness of the pork and peppery bite of the radish. Everybody thinks that pork shoulder has to be cooked for days to be tasty but that's not entirely true. As long as it's cooked quickly and not left to stew in its own juices, pork shoulder is as tender and tasty as loin. In fact, for dishes like this where the meat is cooked on the griddle, I'd even say shoulder surpasses loin.

PREP TIME 20 MINUTES,
PLUS 1 HOUR MARINATING
COOKING TIME 25 MINUTES
—

2 cloves garlic, peeled
 and minced
4cm ginger, peeled and
 grated
75ml light soy sauce
4 x 175g pork shoulder steaks
200g jasmine rice
1 tbsp rice wine vinegar
75g radishes, washed clean
 and thinly sliced
½ iceberg lettuce, shredded
1 tsp sesame seeds, toasted

Put the garlic and ginger in a bowl, pour in the soy sauce and give them a good mix. Add the pork steaks and mix the meat thoroughly into the marinade ingredients – your hands are the most effective tool to do this. Leave to marinate for at least 1 hour.

Whilst the pork is marinating, cover the rice with water and leave to soak for 10 minutes.

Drain the rice and tip into a saucepan (it will need a tight-fitting lid). Pour in 250ml of water and place on a high heat to come to the boil. Once boiling, cover with a lid and turn the heat to minimum. Leave the rice to steam like this for 12 minutes and then turn the heat completely off and leave to sit for 5 minutes. DO NOT stir the rice or lift the lid to have a peek!

When the rice is cooked, stir through a good pinch of salt and the vinegar.

Heat a griddle pan over a high heat and, when smoking hot, lay the pork carefully in the pan and fry for 3–4 minutes on each side, or until you are happy that it is cooked through (it is good for the meat to be charred in places).

Slice the pork and serve on top of a bowl of rice, with the radishes and lettuce and a sprinkling of sesame seeds.

TIP

Keep ginger in the freezer – it will last longer, plus it'll be easier to grate.

KOFTAS WITH CHUNKY FETA SALAD

SERVES 4

This recipe will become a household favourite I assure you. Although on paper the meat is heavily spiced, the final product is in fact subtle enough for the whole family. To make this even speedier, serve the koftas with shop-bought pittas.

PREP TIME 25 MINUTES
COOKING TIME 20 MINUTES

250g self-raising flour,
   plus a little for dusting
1 tsp baking powder
½ lemon, juice only
500g minced lamb
1 egg
75g breadcrumbs
1½ tsp ground cumin
½ tsp ground cinnamon
1 tsp sumac
1 red onion, peeled and
   finely chopped
70g feta, roughly cut into
   1cm pieces
2 large tomatoes, roughly
   chopped into 2cm chunks
½ cucumber, de-seeded
   and roughly chopped
   into 2cm chunks
½ tbsp balsamic vinegar
1 tbsp olive oil
50ml Greek yoghurt
½ small bunch of fresh mint
   leaves, roughly chopped

Tip the flour into a bowl and sprinkle in the baking powder. Pour in about 125ml of water, along with the lemon juice and a good pinch of salt. Mix until the ingredients start to come together. Dust a clean surface with a little flour, tip the dough out and knead for 5 minutes. Drop the dough back into the bowl, cover with clingfilm and leave to rest.

Preheat the grill to maximum.

Mix the lamb, egg, breadcrumbs, spices and half the onion in a bowl, along with a good pinch of both salt and pepper. Give the mixture a good pummelling with your hands to bind it together. Roughly divide into 6 equal amounts and roll into sausage shapes.

Lay the koftas on a lined tray and slide under the preheated grill. Cook for about 6 minutes on each side, or until they are fully cooked through – cut into one and check the meat has turned from pink to cooked brown. Turn off the grill, shut the door and leave them to rest.

Meanwhile, to make the salad, combine the remaining onion, feta, tomatoes and cucumber, along with the vinegar and oil. Toss everything together until well slicked.

Place a griddle pan or non-stick frying pan over a high heat. Roughly divide the dough into 6 balls. Roll them on a floured surface into rough circles about the thickness of a pound coin and then dry fry, one at a time, in the hot griddle or frying pan for 2 minutes on each side.

When all the breads are cooked, spread each one with a little yoghurt along the middle, top with the salad and a kofta and finish with a decorative flourish of the mint.

CHIPOTLE STEAK WRAPS WITH REFRIED BEANS

SERVES 4

What the supermarkets label as 'stewing steak' is often off cuts of premium cuts of meat, so don't be afraid to use it in quick-cook dishes. Just don't let it boil or it will go tough. It can be expensive to buy meat for a large family so make sure to bulk it out with other protein-rich ingredients, such as kidney beans, to fill up the tummies.

PREP TIME 45 MINUTES,
PLUS 15 MINUTES SOAKING
AND 1 HOUR MARINATING
COOKING TIME 25 MINUTES

---

1 dried chipotle chilli
2 cloves garlic, peeled
1 tsp dried oregano
½ orange (roughly 60g),
    zest and juice
400g stewing steak, cut into
    thin ½cm thick slices
1 tbsp butter
1 white onion, peeled and diced
½ small bunch of fresh coriander,
    stalk and leaves separated,
    both finely chopped
1 x 400g tin kidney beans,
    drained and rinsed
300ml chicken stock
1 red chilli, de-seeded and
    finely chopped
½ red onion, peeled and diced
200g passata
1 tbsp vegetable oil
6 large tortillas

Place the chipotle chilli in a bowl and cover with boiling water. Leave to soak for 15 minutes, by which time it should be nicely softened.

Remove half of the seeds from the chipotle chilli (more or less, depending on how hot you like your food) and then roughly chop the pieces and put in a pestle and mortar, along with the garlic, oregano and the orange zest and juice. Grind the ingredients until they become a paste. Tip over the steak and leave to marinate for a minimum of 1 hour.

Whilst the steak is marinating, make the refried beans. Melt the butter in a pan over a medium to high heat and, when hot and bubbling, add the white onion and coriander stalks. Soften the ingredients in the butter for 5 minutes and then add the beans and stock. Bring the liquid to the boil and simmer for 15 minutes, or until the beans are very tender and beginning to fall apart. Give it a good stir to help break up the beans. Season with salt and pepper and then leave to one side.

Mix together the red chilli, red onion and passata, along with a good pinch of both salt and pepper, to make a quick salsa.

When ready to eat, heat the oil in a large frying pan over a high heat. When the oil is smoking, add the marinated beef and stir-fry for 2–3 minutes, or until the meat is just cooked through – do not let it boil or simmer, as that will make it tough.

Serve the beef with the refried beans, salsa and tortillas and get stuck in.

CHAPTER TWO

2

FAMILY FAVOURITES

LUXURY MAC & CHEESE

Fresh bay leaves have a much better flavour than dried ones and so many people grow bay as an ornamental plant. My money-saving tip is to go and nab a leaf from a neighbour! If you can find a different pasta shape more cheaply than macaroni then use that. Always keep cheese in an airtight container, otherwise it will dry out in the fridge and become hard and useless.

PREP TIME 15 MINUTES
COOKING TIME 45 MINUTES

—

600ml milk
outer layers of 1 onion (30g)
1 bay leaf
400g macaroni pasta
80g butter
150g chorizo, cut into 1cm cubes
80g plain flour
1 tsp English mustard powder
50g Cheddar, grated
50g Parmesan, grated
2 tomatoes, sliced thinly
80g breadcrumbs

Pour the milk into a saucepan and add the onion and bay leaf. Bring the milk slowly to the boil, then turn off the heat and leave to sit and infuse.

Bring a large pot of salted water to the boil and, when boiling, add the pasta and cook according to the packet instructions. Drain through a colander and rinse under cold water to cool down completely.

Preheat the oven to 200°C/Gas 6.

Heat the butter in a large saucepan over a medium to high heat. When melted and bubbling, add the chorizo and fry, stirring regularly, for 3 minutes, or until it is completely cooked through.

Sprinkle in the flour and mix with the chorizo and butter to form a roux. Fry, stirring almost constantly, for 1 minute. Reduce the heat to low and stir in a ladleful of the infused milk (dodging the onion and bay leaf), making sure to give it a good beat with the spoon to avoid lumps. When the first ladleful of milk has been absorbed, add another one and stir that in. Continue the process until all of the infused milk has been worked into the roux and you have a silky smooth white sauce. Increase the heat and bring the sauce slowly to the boil to thicken. Reduce the heat again and stir in the mustard powder and cheeses.

Take the pan from the heat and stir in the pasta, making sure all the pieces are well coated in the sauce.

Tip the pasta into an ovenproof dish and arrange the tomato slices on top so they are in one layer. Sprinkle over the breadcrumbs and cook in the preheated oven for 20 minutes, or until the crumbs are crisp and the sauce is bubbling hot.

ROAST TOMATO & ORZO RAGU

SERVES 4

A ragu normally contains meat... This one doesn't but it tastes so good you won't notice. Tomatoes that are going soft and may be past their best are perfect for this recipe as they will be sweeter. Roasting tomatoes intensifies the flavour resulting in a tastier dish.

PREP TIME 15 MINUTES
COOKING TIME 50 MINUTES

250g very ripe tomatoes, roughly chopped into quarters
1 tbsp olive oil
1 onion, peeled and diced
1 clove garlic, peeled and roughly chopped
125g courgette, trimmed and grated
2 celery stalks, washed, trimmed and diced
2 tsp fennel seeds
1 sprig of rosemary
1 tbsp tomato puree
300g orzo pasta
225ml chicken or vegetable stock
½ small bunch of fresh parsley, roughly chopped
25g Parmesan, grated

Preheat the oven to 190°C/Gas 5.

Place the tomatoes on a baking tray, drizzle over roughly half the oil and season generously with salt. Roast in the preheated oven for 20 minutes, or until the tomatoes begin to collapse and colour a little.

Whilst they are roasting, heat the remaining oil in a large, ovenproof casserole over a medium to high heat. When hot, slide in the onion, garlic, courgette and celery. Gently cook the vegetables, stirring regularly, for 10 minutes, by which time they should have broken down and softened.

Add the fennel seeds, rosemary and tomato puree and stir to combine.

Remove the roasted tomatoes from the oven, but don't turn off the heat. Slide the tomatoes and any of their cooking juices straight into the casserole. Stir in the orzo and then pour in the stock. Bring the liquid up to a simmer.

Cover with a lid and bake in the preheated oven for 20 minutes, or until the liquid has been absorbed and the orzo is cooked through.

Let the ingredients sit for 5 minutes and then stir through the parsley and Parmesan just before serving.

GOAN FISH CURRY

Chat up your fishmonger to get the best prices – you'll often find they are cheaper than the supermarket and far more knowledgeable. You don't have to buy expensive curry pastes – learn to make them yourself and save a fortune. Don't overcook the fish! Too many people think they don't like fish, but it's just because they've overcooked it through paranoia.

PREP TIME 15 MINUTES,
PLUS 45 MINUTES SOAKING
COOKING TIME 40 MINUTES
—

150g red lentils
1 small bunch of fresh basil
1 small bunch of fresh coriander,
    leaves and stalks separated
2 cloves garlic, peeled and
    roughly chopped
3cm ginger, peeled and
    roughly chopped
zest of 1 lime
1 tsp chilli powder
1 tbsp vegetable oil
1 star anise
1 onion, peeled and diced
700ml fish stock
400g coley, cut into large
    4cm chunks

Tip the lentils into a bowl, cover with water and leave to soak for 45 minutes. After the soaking time, drain through a sieve and leave to drain totally.

Place the basil (leaves and stalks), coriander (just stalks), garlic, ginger, lime zest and chilli powder in a food processor and blitz until smooth, adding a little water, if needed, to get it going.

Heat the oil in a large casserole dish over a medium to high heat. When hot, add the star anise and the onion and fry for 5 minutes. Add the curry paste and 'cook out', stirring almost constantly, for 4 minutes.

Pour in the stock and bring to the boil.

Add the soaked lentils and simmer for 20 minutes, or until the lentils are just cooked through.

Add the fish pieces, pouring in a little extra water, if needed. Bring back up to a simmer and cook for a further 10 minutes.

Roughly chop the coriander leaves and stir through the curry before serving.

TIP

Keep hold of the onion peelings to flavour things like white sauce.

BAKED KEDGEREE

SERVES 4

Such a warming bowl of comfort, perfectly flavoured with the subtle smokiness of smoked haddock. Using risotto rice gives the dish a rich, almost creamy texture without having to add any cheese or cream. Mixing fish and chicken stock cubes makes for a less fishy flavour to the dish. If you don't have an ovenproof casserole dish, then cook the mixture in a normal saucepan and then transfer to an ovenproof dish, cover with tin foil and bake for 5 minutes more than the recipe states.

PREP TIME 10 MINUTES
COOKING TIME 45 MINUTES

35g butter
2 rashers smoked streaky bacon, cut into 1cm thick strips
1 onion, peeled and diced
2 celery stalks, washed and diced
1 clove garlic, peeled and finely chopped
1½ tsp mild curry powder
300g risotto rice (arborio)
250g skinless smoked haddock, cut into 1cm cubes
½ chicken stock cube
½ fish stock cube
300ml semi-skimmed milk
4 eggs
1 tsp finely chopped chives
a pinch of cayenne pepper

Preheat the oven to 180°C/Gas 4.

Heat the butter in an ovenproof casserole dish over a medium to high heat and, when it has melted and is bubbling, add the bacon, onion and celery and fry, stirring regularly, for 5 minutes, or until the onion has softened.

Reduce the heat to medium and add both the garlic and curry powder and continue to stir and fry for another minute before shaking in the rice and stirring to combine with the rest of the ingredients. Fry the rice for 1 minute, stirring to slick it with the oil in the pan, then gently drop in the haddock and crumble in the two halves of stock cube.

Pour in the milk, along with 400ml of water, season well with salt and pepper, and bring the liquid up to the boil, whilst continuously stirring the mix. Cover with a lid and transfer to the preheated oven and bake for 15 minutes.

Remove the dish from the oven and give the mixture a good stir. Make 4 small hollows in the surface of the risotto and crack an egg into each one. Slide the dish back into the oven uncovered and bake for a further 4 minutes, or until the white of each egg is cooked through but the yolk is still a little runny.

Sprinkle the kedgeree with chives and the cayenne pepper to serve.

TIP

Store your onions in tights to make them last longer – tie a knot between each one for individual storage.

SMOKED HADDOCK FISHCAKES

SERVES 4

Smoked haddock gives you so much flavour for the price of it. Maris Piper, King Edward, Desiree, who knows which is the best potato to buy? We do: the cheapest ones that are firm to touch. Just make a bit more mash the night before and you're half way to making your fishcake.

PREP TIME 15 MINUTES
COOKING TIME 30 MINUTES

600g potatoes, peeled and
   cut into large 4cm chunks
275g smoked haddock
250ml milk
1 bay leaf
1 tbsp vegetable oil
½ onion, peeled and diced
½ x 400g tin chopped tomatoes
1 tbsp dark brown sugar
1 tbsp red wine vinegar
1 tsp English mustard
25g breadcrumbs
2 tbsp plain flour
130g butter
5 eggs
1 tbsp white wine vinegar
100g baby spinach

Boil the potatoes in a large pan until completely tender. Drain, leave to steam dry for 5 minutes and then mash until smooth.

Place the haddock in a saucepan and pour over the milk. Add enough water to cover the fish completely. Add the bay leaf and bring the liquid to the boil. Turn the heat down to its lowest setting, cover with a lid and then leave the fish to poach gently for 10 minutes.

After 10 minutes, take the fish from the liquid and, using a knife and fork, flake the flesh into the bowl of mashed potato, discarding any skin and bones along the way.

Heat the oil in a small saucepan over a medium to high heat and, when hot, add the onion and fry, stirring regularly, for 6 minutes, or until very soft. Add the tomatoes and bring up to a simmer. Stir in the sugar and red wine vinegar and cook for 4 minutes, then blitz until smooth. This is your homemade ketchup. Leave to one side to cool to room temperature.

Spoon about 3 tablespoons of the fish poaching liquid into the fish mixture and also add the mustard and breadcrumbs, along with a good pinch of both salt and pepper. Shape the mixture into 4 large fishcakes and dust in flour. Leave to set in the fridge whilst you make the hollandaise.

Melt 100g of the butter in a small pan and put to one side. Separate one of the eggs, keeping the white for another day, and plopping the yolk into a large bowl. Pour the white wine vinegar in with the egg yolk and then place the bowl over a medium pan filled with simmering water. Make sure the base of the bowl doesn't come into contact with the surface of the water. Whisk the vinegar and yolk together for 2 minutes, or until light and fluffy. Take the pan off the heat and begin to add the melted butter gradually, whisking almost constantly. Once all of the butter has been incorporated, continue to whisk off the heat until you reach a thick hollandaise sauce. Whisk in a few spoons of warm water if the sauce is too thick, season with salt and pepper and leave to one side.

Heat half the remaining butter in a pan over a medium heat and, when hot, fry the fishcakes for 3 minutes on each side, until golden brown and hot through. Put on a plate to one side.

Meanwhile, bring a pan of water to the boil and, when simmering, crack in the remaining 4 eggs and reduce the heat right down so the water is barely bubbling. Poach the eggs like this for 4–5 minutes for a soft yolk.

Add the remaining butter to the pan used to fry the fishcakes and, when hot and melted, wilt the spinach.

Serve each fishcake on top of some wilted spinach, topped with a poached egg and finished with the hollandaise sauce. Serve the homemade ketchup on the side.

TIP

Don't store leftover tinned tomatoes in the can as they can create toxins that make the tomatoes go off quicker. Instead, tip the leftovers into an airtight plastic container.

CHICKEN & LEEK PIE SERVES **6**

Chicken thighs are so very cheap and easy to cook. Don't even think about throwing the green part of the leek away, just be sure to give it a thorough wash. Filo pastry is a brilliant alternative to puff or shortcrust.

PREP TIME 30 MINUTES
COOKING TIME 1 HOUR
——

40ml vegetable oil
900g chicken thighs, bone in and skin on
1 litre chicken stock
50g butter
150g leek, washed and finely sliced
1 onion, peeled and diced
150g mushrooms, brushed clean and roughly chopped
60g plain flour
50ml crème fraiche
30g Parmesan, grated
1 small bunch of fresh parsley, roughly chopped
150g filo pastry, about 4 sheets
300g carrots, boiled, to serve

Heat 30ml of the oil in a large saucepan and brown the chicken. This should take about 10 minutes; make sure the thighs are dark golden brown all over.

Pour the stock over the chicken, adding a little more water, if needed, to cover the thighs.

Simmer the chicken for 30 minutes, or until they are cooked through and tender. Remove from the pan and leave to cool a little. Reserve 750ml of the cooking liquid.

When you can handle the chicken comfortably, strip away the skin and discard it. Flake the meat from the bone and keep to one side. Throw away the bones as they have served their purpose.

Melt the butter in a large saucepan over a medium to high heat and, when melted and bubbling, add the leek and onion and fry, stirring regularly, for about 8 minutes, or until the vegetables have softened.

Increase the heat to maximum and add the mushrooms. Continue to stir and fry for another 3 minutes.

Reduce the heat to medium and sprinkle in the flour, stirring as you go. When the flour is fully incorporated, pour a ladleful of the cooking liquid into the pan and stir to incorporate. Continue to stir and add the liquid until all of it has been incorporated and you have a smooth, silky sauce. Taste and season with salt and pepper.

Take the pan from the heat and stir in the cooked chicken, crème fraiche, Parmesan and parsley. Tip the mixture into a pie dish and leave to cool just a little.

Preheat the oven to 190°C/Gas 5.

Take one sheet of filo at a time and scrunch it up a little before plonking it directly on top of the cooled pie filling. Repeat the process with the remaining sheets of pastry until the whole pie is covered.

Brush the pastry with the remaining oil and bake the pie in the oven for 25 minutes, or until the filo has turned crisp and the pie filling is piping hot.

Serve with simply boiled carrots on the side.

TIP

Even though things like olive oil and condiments have a long shelf life, this often reduces greatly once they're opened, so if it's something you'll only use occasionally, buy a smaller bottle.

CHICKEN TAGINE

Bone-in and skin-on chicken is the best way to buy it – not only is it cheaper, but it is also tastier. Stop buying skinless breasts and get on the thighway (sorry, I couldn't help myself). For some reason we all think spices are very expensive, but they're really economical in terms of flavour to cost.

PREP TIME 15 MINUTES
COOKING TIME 35 MINUTES

800ml chicken stock
275g couscous
a few strands of saffron
1 tbsp olive oil
750g chicken thighs,
   bone in and skin on
2 onions, peeled and diced
1 tsp turmeric
1 tsp ground coriander
20g preserved lemon,
   cut into small slices
½ cucumber, diced
1 small bunch of fresh
   coriander, chopped
1 small bunch of fresh
   mint, chopped

Bring the stock to the boil and tip the couscous into a serving bowl. Pour 350ml of boiling stock over the couscous, give it a stir and then cover with clingfilm and leave to rehydrate.

Add the saffron to the remaining hot stock and leave to infuse.

Meanwhile, heat the oil in a large casserole dish over a medium to high heat and, when hot, brown the chicken all over. This should take about 10 minutes – you're aiming for a deep golden colour. Remove the browned chicken and keep to one side.

Reduce the heat to medium, slide in the onions and fry for 5 minutes, or until they are starting to soften and turn translucent. Add the turmeric and coriander and fry, stirring almost constantly, for a minute or so. Nestle the chicken among the onion and add the lemon slices.

Pour over the saffron-infused stock and bring to the boil. Cover with a cocked lid and simmer for 30 minutes, or until you're happy the chicken is cooked through.

Whilst the chicken is cooking, take the clingfilm off the couscous, fluff up with a fork and add the cucumber, half the coriander and mint, along with a good pinch of both salt and pepper. Give the whole lot a good mix.

When the chicken is ready, sprinkle the tagine with the remaining herbs and serve both dishes together.

CHICKEN PROVENCAL

SERVES 4

Lentils were so often the scorn of the carnivore, an insignificant pulse that was consumed by hippies and vegetarians – how things have changed. Lentils are now considered a superfood: not only are they high in tummy-filling protein and rammed full of gut-cleansing fibre but they are also incredibly tasty with a satisfying, gently nutty flavour.

PREP TIME: 15 MINUTES,
PLUS 30 MINUTES SOAKING
COOKING TIME: 40 MINUTES

———

175g puy lentils
1 tbsp sunflower oil
750g chicken thighs,
    bone in and skin on
3 rashers smoked streaky
    bacon cut into 1cm slices
2 onions, peeled and diced
2 celery stalks, washed and
    finely chopped
3 cloves garlic, peeled and
    finely chopped
2 sprigs of fresh thyme
1 bay leaf
300g tomatoes, roughly
    chopped into 3cm chunks
600ml chicken stock
½ small bunch of fresh
    parsley, roughly chopped

Tip the lentils into a large bowl, cover with water and leave to soak for 30 minutes.

Heat the oil in a large casserole dish over a medium to high heat. When hot carefully lay the chicken thighs in the dish, skin side down. Fry for about 4 minutes on the skin side, or until they are a deep golden brown, then flip them over and fry for a further 2 minutes on the flesh side. Remove them to a plate.

Place the bacon, onions and celery in the pan and fry, stirring regularly, for 5 minutes. Add the garlic, thyme and bay, and continue to fry for a further 2 minutes. Stir in the tomatoes and cook, stirring regularly, for 3–4 minutes, or until the tomatoes start to break down a little.

Drain the lentils and then stir into the pan. Carefully lay the chicken thighs on top of the lentil mix, pour in the stock, season with a good pinch of salt and pepper, and bring up to the boil. Cover with a lid and simmer for 40 minutes, or until the thighs are cooked through and the lentils are nice and tender.

Stir in the parsley to serve.

TIP

Store tomatoes with their stems down in order to stop moisture getting in. If you don't, they will go bad more quickly.

SPICED CHICKEN & BULGUR WHEAT

SERVES
4

Bulgur wheat is one of those mysterious ingredients that looks like it could be quite nice and healthy, but we're not too sure how to cook it. Look no further – in this recipe the bulgur wheat soaks up the flavour of the chicken, resulting in a delicious, satisfying meal for everyone.

PREP TIME 15 MINUTES
COOKING TIME 40 MINUTES

1 tbsp vegetable oil
750g chicken thighs,
    skin on and bone in
1 onion, peeled and diced
100g carrots, peeled and diced
2 celery stalks, washed and
    diced, plus a small handful of
    celery leaves
2 cloves garlic, peeled
    and finely chopped
1 tsp ground cinnamon
½ tsp ground turmeric
1 tbsp tomato puree
175g bulgur wheat
2 tbsp raisins
600ml chicken stock
60g feta

Heat the oil in a large saucepan over a medium to high heat. When hot, add the chicken thighs, skin side down, and fry for about 4 minutes, or until the skin has turned a golden brown colour. Flip the thighs and cook for another 2 minutes, and then remove them to a plate.

Add the onion, carrots and celery to the pan and fry, stirring regularly, for about 5 minutes, or until the vegetables begin to soften. Reduce the heat a little if they start to catch.

Add the garlic and continue to fry for a further minute.

Sprinkle in the spices and add the tomato puree. Fry, stirring almost continuously, for 1 minute.

Pour in the bulgur wheat and raisins and stir to combine. Nestle the chicken thighs, skin side up, back into the pan. Pour over the stock and bring up to the boil. Cover with a lid and cook for 20–25 minutes, or until the chicken thighs are cooked through.

Remove the lid and sprinkle with the celery leaves and crumble over the feta before serving.

TIP

Bulgur wheat is a great ingredient to throw into a soup or a salad to bulk it up.

CHICKEN KIEVS SERVES 4

Don't buy readymade kievs – they're so easy to make yourself. Frozen chicken is the cheapest way of eating chicken breast. Use almost any herb or spice to flavour your butter – it can sit in the fridge and be pulled out whenever needed. And if you have any butter left over, then use it to flavour your Cod Fillets (page 39) and you'll have an even speedier supper.

PREP TIME 20 MINUTES
COOKING TIME 20 MINUTES
—

50g butter, softened
1 clove garlic, peeled and
    finely minced
1 tbsp finely chopped fresh
    chives
1 small bunch of fresh parsley,
    finely chopped
4 chicken breasts
2 tbsp flour
2 eggs
80g breadcrumbs
40ml vegetable oil
1 onion, peeled and diced
1 tbsp tomato puree
1 bay leaf
200g long grain rice
500ml vegetable or chicken stock

Preheat the oven to 200°C/Gas 6.

Place the softened butter in a bowl and add the garlic, chives and half the parsley, as well as a good pinch of both salt and pepper. Beat the ingredients together until you reach a smooth mix. Dollop the butter on to a piece of clingfilm, roll up into a sausage shape and leave to firm up in the fridge.

Cut a small slit into the thick side of each chicken breast. Wiggle the knife about a bit to make a small pocket. Cut the butter into 4 roughly equal pieces and push into the pockets.

Tip the flour on to a plate, crack and whisk the eggs on to another plate and scatter the breadcrumbs on a third.

Take each breast one at a time and dust in the flour, dip in the egg and then finally roll in the breadcrumbs. Repeat the process with the remaining stuffed breasts.

When all breasts are crumbed all over, heat half the oil in a large frying pan over a medium to high heat and, when hot, fry the breasts for 2–3 minutes on each side, or until lightly golden. Transfer the browned breasts to a baking tray and keep to one side.

Heat the remaining oil in a large, ovenproof casserole over a medium to high heat and, when hot, fry the onion for 6–8 minutes, or until softened. Add the tomato puree and bay leaf and fry for a further minute. Add the rice, slicking it with the other ingredients, before pouring in the stock. Bring the liquid to the boil, cover with a lid and then place in the preheated oven.

When the rice has had 5 minutes, slide the tray with the kievs into the oven as well and cook both for a further 10 minutes.

Serve sprinkled with the remaining chopped parsley.

CHICKEN & BASIL
BAKED RISOTTO SERVES 4

The main piece of advice for this recipe is to use breasts from a whole chicken – the thighs and the carcass can be used for another dish and buying a whole chicken is cheaper than buying breasts. If you want to reduce the cost even more, then leave out the chorizo. This recipe takes advantage of both the stalks and leaves of the herb.

PREP TIME 20 MINUTES
COOKING TIME 45 MINUTES

---

2 tbsp olive oil
1 leek, white only, chopped
   up (roughly 100g)
45g chorizo, cut into cubes
1 small bunch of fresh basil,
   leaves and stalks separated,
   both chopped
300g risotto rice
a few strands of saffron
1 bay leaf
900ml chicken stock
2 chicken breasts, cut from
   a whole chicken, and sliced
   into 1cm strips (roughly 275g)

Preheat the oven to 180°C/Gas 4.

Heat the oil in a heavy based saucepan and chuck in the leek and chorizo. Fry for 2 minutes then add the basil stalks, rice, saffron and bay leaf, and keep frying for another minute, stirring almost constantly.

Pour in the stock and bring to the boil. Cover with a lid, then slide the dish into the preheated oven and bake for 15 minutes.

Take the risotto out of the oven and stir in the chicken. Cover with the lid and return to the oven to cook for a further 15 minutes.

Garnish with the basil leaves before serving.

TIP

Save the green part of the leek to add to the base of a soup another day.

CAJUN CHICKEN WITH POMEGRANATE COUSCOUS

SERVES 4

Who would have thought the humble cornflake could be elevated to such a grown-up, savoury dish? Cooking is very much based on imagination and confidence, so next time you're stuck for an idea, try thinking outside the (cereal) box.

PREP TIME 25 MINUTES
COOKING TIME 15 MINUTES

100g couscous
2 tbsp raisins
400ml chicken stock
4 chicken thighs, bone in and skin on
100g cornflakes
1½ tsp ground paprika
1½ tsp ground cumin
1 egg white
4 tbsp plain flour
sunflower oil, for frying
1 tbsp olive oil
2 large tomatoes, roughly chopped into small pieces (roughly 100g)
½ cucumber, de-seeded and diced
2 spring onions, finely sliced
50g pomegranate seeds
1 small bunch of fresh parsley, chopped

Tip the couscous into a large bowl, add the raisins and pour the hot stock over them. Cover the bowl with clingfilm and leave to sit for 10 minutes, or until cool.

Remove the skin and bone from the thighs and then bash the meat with a rolling pin between two pieces of clingfilm until thin.

Bash the cornflakes with a rolling pin in a sandwich bag until they become small pieces, then add the spices to the bag, shake and tip on to a plate.

Lightly beat the egg white in a small bowl and measure the flour into a separate shallow bowl.

Take each chicken thigh one at a time and dip in the flour, then the egg and then press into the spiced cornflakes.

Heat a little sunflower oil in a large frying pan (you might need to use two medium ones) and gently fry all the chicken thighs together for about 10 minutes, turning halfway through.

While the chicken is cooking, fluff up the couscous with a fork, pour in the olive oil, then add the tomatoes, cucumber, spring onions, pomegranate seeds and parsley, keeping some parsley back to garnish the finished dish.

Serve up and chow down.

TIP

Don't store tomatoes in plastic bags – they ripen faster that way and go off quicker.

PULLED CHICKEN FAJITAS

Slow cooking helps the meat take on huge amounts of flavour, whilst rendering its texture deliciously unctuous and tender. Chicken thighs with the bone in are filled with flavour. We've opted to remove the skin, as it can turn a little flabby. Don't store leftover tinned tomatoes in the can as they can create toxins that make the tomatoes go off more quickly.

PREP TIME 15 MINUTES,
PLUS 60 MINUTES MARINATING
COOKING TIME 90 MINUTES
—

3 red onions, peeled and
   roughly diced
1 orange, juice and zest
3 cloves garlic, peeled and
   roughly diced
½ tsp dried oregano
½ tsp dried thyme
½ tsp sweet smoked paprika
½ x 400g tin chopped tomatoes
750g chicken thighs, bone
   in, skin removed
1 tbsp butter
1 white onion, peeled and diced
1 small bunch of fresh coriander,
   leaves and stalks separated
   and roughly chopped
1 x 400g tin kidney beans
250ml chicken stock
250g tomatoes, roughly chopped
juice of 1 lime
8 tortilla wraps
1 iceberg lettuce, shredded
300g Cheddar, grated
200ml soured cream

Place 200g of the red onion, the juice and zest of the orange, the garlic, oregano, thyme, smoked paprika and tinned tomatoes into a food processor, along with a good pinch of both salt and pepper and blitz until smooth.

Lay the chicken thighs into a large roasting tray and pour the tomato mix over the top. Leave the chicken to marinate for about 1 hour.

Preheat the oven to 170°C/Gas 3.

Once the chicken has marinated, roast in the preheated oven for 90 minutes, by which time the chicken will be tender and fully cooked through. If the top of the chicken is starting to burn, then cover with some tin foil.

Remove the chicken from the oven and, using a knife and fork, pull out the bones and discard. Roughly tear up the meat with your knife and fork, cover and keep the meat warm until ready to serve.

Whilst the meat is cooking, heat the butter in a large saucepan over a medium to high heat and, when melted and bubbling, add the white onion and coriander stalks. Cook the ingredients together for about 8 minutes, stirring regularly. Drain the kidney beans and add to the saucepan with the stock. Bring the liquid to the boil and then simmer the ingredients for about 20 minutes, or until the beans are soft enough to break up.

Meanwhile, make a quick salsa by mixing together the remaining red onion, tomatoes, lime juice and some salt and pepper. Add half the coriander leaves and stir these through, too.

When ready to eat, heat up the tortilla wraps in the microwave or wrap them in foil and place in the oven.

Serve the pulled chicken, refried beans, salsa, shredded lettuce, cheese and soured cream all together and let people make up their own fajitas.

CHICKEN & SAUSAGE TRAYBAKE

Chicken thighs and sausage meat all together in a one-tray dinner for all the family – sounds too good to be true? Well, it isn't. This recipe is bound to become a firm family favourite that you'll be cooking up at least once a week, not only because it's tasty, but also because it's so easy to make.

PREP TIME 20 MINUTES
COOKING TIME 40 MINUTES

——

1½ tbsp vegetable oil
750g chicken thighs,
   bone in and skin on
600g potatoes, scrubbed clean,
   cut into 6 wedges each
2 red onions, peeled and
   cut into wedges
3 sprigs of fresh thyme
200g sausage meat
250g tomatoes, roughly
   chopped into 4cm chunks
80g baby spinach

Preheat the oven to 220°C/Gas 7.

Pour the oil into a large roasting tray and slide it into the preheated oven to heat up for 6 minutes. When the oil is hot, take the tray out of the oven and lay the chicken thighs, skin side down, in the hot oil and scatter the potatoes around the chicken – try to keep everything in a single layer. Return the tray to the oven and roast for 15 minutes.

Carefully remove the hot tray from the oven and flip the chicken and potatoes. Scatter over the onion wedges and slide the thyme leaves from their stalks and sprinkle over the traybake – and then chuck in the stalks, too. Return the tray to the oven for a further 5 minutes.

Whilst the chicken is roasting away, roll the sausage meat into 8 roughly similar-sized balls – they will be small, but that is good.

Take the roasting tray out of the oven and give all the ingredients a good mix around. Place the sausage meatballs and tomatoes amongst the chicken, potatoes and onions. Give the whole lot a generous seasoning of salt and pepper, and then return the tray to the oven for a final 20 minutes.

Remove from the oven, scatter over the spinach, mixing it in with the other cooked ingredients very roughly and then serve up straight from the tray.

TIP

Sausage meat is a little bit cheaper than fully formed sausages and is exactly the same meat – it just doesn't have its shirt on.

CHICKEN WINGS WITH APPLESLAW

SERVES 4

Wings are the cheapest, yet very much the tastiest cut of chicken available. Admittedly you have to put in a bit of effort and give yourself a wipe down after but jump those hurdles and a cheap and tasty dish is on its way to your tummy. These wings are a bit spicy, but the apple slaw acts as the perfect cooling companion.

PREP TIME 20 MINUTES
COOKING TIME 30 MINUTES

2 tbsp vegetable oil
½ tsp onion salt
½ tsp celery salt
2 tsp sweet smoked paprika
½ tsp cayenne pepper
1.8kg chicken wings
3 tbsp mayonnaise
1 lemon, juice only
½ tbsp Dijon mustard
1 green apple, core removed
   and sliced
¼ red cabbage, core removed
   and leaves shredded
1 red onion, peeled and
   finely sliced
125g carrots, peeled and grated
thick cut bread, to serve

Preheat the oven to 200°C/Gas 6. Slide a roasting tray into the oven so it can heat up, too.

In a large bowl, mix together the oil, onion salt, celery salt, paprika and cayenne pepper, along with a good grinding of fresh pepper. Toss in the chicken wings and coat them in the spiced oil.

Carefully remove the hot tray from the oven and place the chicken on to it.

Roast the wings in the oven for about 25 minutes, turning once, until they are golden brown and cooked through.

Whilst the wings are cooking, mix together the mayonnaise, lemon juice and mustard until they reach a smooth consistency. Add all the prepared fruit and vegetables and give the whole lot a good toss to coat.

Serve the appleslaw with the chicken wings and some good chunks of bread to soak up the flavours.

TOAD IN THE HOLE WITH CARAMELISED ONION GRAVY

SERVES 4

When using herbs such as thyme, don't throw away the stalks – they are full of flavour – add them to your dish, too. Just be sure to fish them out before serving. You could use traditional sausages, rather than sausage meat, if you prefer.

PREP TIME 20 MINUTES
COOKING TIME 50 MINUTES

500g sausage meat
1½ tbsp sunflower oil
2 eggs
250ml milk
125g plain flour, plus 1 tbsp
1 large swede (roughly 300g), peeled and chopped into 2–3cm chunks
275g carrots, peeled and chopped into 2–3cm chunks
2 tbsp butter
1 large onion, peeled and finely sliced
150ml red wine
2 sprigs of thyme
400ml beef stock

Preheat the oven to 220°C/Gas 7.

Roll the sausage meat into golfball-sized pieces and place them in a roasting dish (20 x 15cm). Drizzle with the oil, slide into the preheated oven and roast for 10 minutes.

Whilst the sausages are cooking, crack the eggs into a jug and beat in the milk. Tip 125g of the flour into a large bowl and gradually whisk in the milk and egg mixture until you reach a smooth batter. Stir in a good amount of both salt and pepper. Pour the batter back into the jug.

Put a pan of water on to boil.

When the sausages have had their 10 minutes, take the tray from the oven and, working quickly and carefully, gently pour the batter into the hot tray. The balls may move around a little as they are swept about by the batter, but don't worry. Slide the dish straight back into the oven and roast for a further 10 minutes, before reducing the temperature to 170°C/Gas 3 and cooking for another 30 minutes, or until the batter is cooked through.

Whilst the toad in the hole is in the oven, carefully add the swede and carrots to the pot of boiling water. Simmer for about 15 minutes, or until totally soft, and then drain through a colander. Toss the cooked vegetables in the colander to release the steam and then tip back into the pot. Add 1 tablespoon of the butter, plus a good pinch of both salt and pepper. Mash the ingredients together, then cover with a lid to keep the vegetables warm until ready to serve.

To make the gravy, heat the remaining butter in a saucepan over a medium to high heat and, when melted, add the onion. Fry, stirring regularly, for 10 minutes, or until the onion is just starting to soften. Turn up the heat, add the wine and the thyme and continue to cook for a further 2 minutes until the wine has reduced by roughly three quarters.

Sprinkle the remaining flour into the gravy saucepan and quickly beat it into the other ingredients. Fry the mixture for 1 minute, stirring continuously. Take the pan off the heat and stir in one third of the stock until smooth. Return the pan to the heat, and pour in the remaining stock. Bring the liquid to the boil and simmer for 1 minute.

By now your toad should be ready, so remove from the oven, portion up and serve with a generous mound of vegetable mash and a slug of onion gravy.

TIP

It's a good idea to portion up minced meat before freezing it – that way you can just take out and defrost/cook the amount you actually need.

BANGERS WITH CAULIFLOWER & BUTTER BEAN MASH

SERVES 4

People used to think of cauliflower as the stinky vegetable served up by dinner ladies to torture school children. Well, not any more – cauliflower is hip and has become a part of the healthy revolution. Most importantly, it's also cheap. You may have seen it made into rice and couscous, but here we've combined it with butter beans to turn it into mash.

PREP TIME 20 MINUTES
COOKING TIME 35 MINUTES

12 sausages
1 cauliflower (roughly 600g), stalk and florets, roughly chopped
1 x 400g tin butter beans, drained
20g Parmesan, grated
1 tbsp butter
1 onion, peeled and thinly sliced
1 bay leaf
1 sprig of rosemary
1 tbsp plain flour
500ml beef stock

Turn the grill on to maximum and put a large pot of water on to boil.

Arrange the sausages on a grill tray and slide under the hot grill. Cook for about 15 minutes, turning a couple of times to ensure even cooking, or until the sausages are cooked through.

Meanwhile, when the water has come to the boil, carefully drop in the cauliflower and cook for about 10 minutes, or until tender. Add the beans and continue to cook for another 4 minutes, by which time the ingredients should be very soft. Drain through a colander and give them a shake to remove as much liquid as possible. Tip back into the saucepan, season with salt and pepper and add the Parmesan. Mash the ingredients together to form a rough mash. Cover with a lid to keep warm until ready to serve.

Whilst the sausages and cauliflower are cooking, heat the butter in a saucepan over a medium heat. When the butter has melted and is bubbling, add the onion and cook, stirring regularly, for about 5 minutes. Drop in the bay leaf and rosemary and continue cooking until the onion is lightly coloured and very soft. Stir in the flour and cook for a further minute.

Take the onion pan from the heat and stir in a third of the stock. Keep stirring until the mixture is smooth, and then stir in a second third of stock. Place the pan back on the heat and pour in the last third of stock, stirring again until smooth. Slowly bring the gravy up to the boil and simmer until thickened.

Serve the mash topped with the sausages and lashings of gravy.

SAUSAGE & ORZO RAGU

The indomitable sausage is everyone's favourite; from dad to daughter, nobody can say no to the humble banger. This recipe combines sausages with the very moreish orzo pasta, which is basically pasta disguised as rice, which soaks up flavour.

PREP TIME 10 MINUTES
COOKING TIME 40 MINUTES

——

1½ tbsp olive oil

1 onion, peeled and diced

150g courgette, trimmed and diced

2 celery stalks, washed and diced

2 tsp fennel seeds

1 large sprig of rosemary

300g sausage meat

20g tomato puree

250g orzo pasta

500ml chicken stock

½ small bunch of fresh parsley, roughly chopped, to serve

Preheat the oven to 180°C/Gas 4.

Heat the oil in a large, ovenproof casserole dish over a medium to high heat. When hot, add the onion, courgette and celery and cook, stirring regularly for 5 minutes, or until all the vegetables are beginning to soften.

Turn the heat up to maximum and add the fennel seeds, rosemary and sausage meat. Fry quickly, breaking up the meat with a wooden spoon until it starts to brown.

Add the tomato puree and tip in the orzo. Continue to fry for 1 more minute.

Pour in the stock and bring up to the boil.

Season with salt and pepper, cover with a lid and bake in the preheated oven for 25 minutes, or until the orzo is soft and has absorbed the stock.

Stir through the parsley and serve.

TIP

You can reinvigorate limp celery by dropping it upright into a jar of cold water – this will crisp it up again. This also works for broccoli, cauliflower, asparagus, lettuce and spinach.

PORK & TURKEY SAGE MEATBALLS

SERVES 4

It is a wonderful Italian tradition to mix together two different types of mince for a recipe. We're carrying on the tradition with these delicious meatballs that combine the flavour and economy of minced turkey with the rich texture of minced pork all wrapped up in a delicious tomato sauce, yum.

PREP TIME 20 MINUTES
COOKING TIME 35 MINUTES

175g minced turkey
175g minced pork
80g breadcrumbs
1 egg
2 cloves garlic, peeled
   and finely chopped
6 sage leaves, finely chopped
grating of nutmeg
1 tbsp olive oil
1 red onion, peeled and diced
1 tbsp tomato puree
1 tbsp balsamic vinegar
1 x 400g tin chopped tomatoes
350g penne pasta
1 small bunch of basil, roughly
   chopped, stalks and all

Place both the minced meats in a large bowl and add the breadcrumbs, egg, half the garlic, all the sage and nutmeg, as well as a good pinch of salt and pepper. Get your hands stuck in and work the mixture until the ingredients are well mixed and binding together.

Roughly divide the mixture into quarters and then make 4 golfball-sized meatballs from each quarter so that you end up with 16 meatballs altogether. Place them on a plate, cover and keep in the fridge until ready to use.

Heat the oil in a large saucepan or high-sided frying pan over a medium to high heat and, when hot, add the onion and remaining garlic. Fry for 4 minutes, stirring regularly, until the onion has softened. Add the tomato puree and continue to fry for another minute.

Crank up the heat to maximum and, when you reach a good sizzle, pour in the vinegar, which will bubble up and evaporate to almost nothing. Follow quickly with the tomatoes. Half fill the empty tomato tin with water and add this to the pan. Bring to the boil and simmer for 2 minutes.

Remove the meatballs from the fridge and carefully lower them into the sauce. Bring the pan back up to a simmer and cook for 5 minutes. Carefully turn the meatballs over and cook for a further 7–8 minutes, or until you are certain they are cooked through. (You can check this by cutting one of the balls open – the meat should have turned from raw pink to cooked brown.)

Whilst the meatballs are bubbling away, bring a pan of water to the boil and cook the penne according to the packet instructions.

Serve the pasta topped with the meatballs and a scattering of the basil.

RICH BEAN STEW

SERVES **6**

Pulses and legumes are a brilliant source of protein that taste great, are cheap and also make your tummy full. If you have any of stew left over, use it to fill cannelloni for an easy and delicious meal on another day (page 141).

PREP TIME 15 MINUTES
COOKING TIME 35 MINUTES

1½ tbsp vegetable oil
2 rashers smoked bacon,
    cut into 1cm slices
1 onion, peeled and diced
100g carrots, peeled and diced
1 celery stalk, washed and diced
375g minced pork
2 tbsp tomato puree
6 sage leaves, finely chopped
1 sprig of rosemary
5cm orange peel
300ml chicken stock
1 x 400g tin butter beans,
    drained and rinsed
1 x 400g tin kidney beans,
    drained and rinsed
80g breadcrumbs
20g Parmesan, grated

Heat the oil in a large saucepan over a medium to high heat and, when hot, add the bacon, onion, carrot and celery and stir-fry for 5 minutes, or until the vegetables are just starting to soften.

Turn the heat up to maximum and add the pork. Fry, breaking the pork up with a spoon as it cooks.

Add the tomato puree, sage, rosemary and orange peel and continue to fry for 2 minutes. Pour in the stock and bring to a simmer.

Preheat the oven to 190°C/Gas 5.

Tip the beans into the pan and simmer everything together for 10 minutes with the lid on and then a further 10 minutes with the lid off.

Tip into a baking dish, top with the breadcrumbs and Parmesan and bake in the preheated oven for 25 minutes, or until the mixture is bubbling and the crumbs have turned golden brown.

TIP

Everybody should be required to have tomato puree in their cupboard. It is the Swiss Army knife of ingredients.

PORK CHOPS WITH CREAMY SPRING GREENS & ROOT MASH

SERVES 4

Pork continues to be astoundingly cheap and versatile, compared to almost any other meat available in the supermarket, but it doesn't compromise on either flavour or texture. In fact, pork chops are one of the tastiest and easiest cuts of meat to cook at home. You'll find loin chops both on and off the bone; there is very little difference in price so go with whichever.

PREP TIME 15 MINUTES
COOKING TIME 25 MINUTES

- 300g swede, peeled and roughly cut into 3cm chunks
- 3 large carrots, peeled and roughly cut into 3cm chunks
- 2 tbsp butter
- 4 pork chops (roughly 200g each)
- 1 clove garlic, peeled and finely chopped
- 1 sprig of thyme
- 400g spring greens, thick stalks removed
- 40ml double cream

Put a large pan of water on to boil and, when bubbling, add the swede and carrots. Simmer for about 20 minutes, or until the vegetables are very soft. Drain through a colander, giving them a good shake to remove as much excess liquid as possible. Tip back into their cooking pot, add half the butter, a good pinch of both salt and pepper, and then mash the vegetables together.

Whilst the roots are cooking, preheat the grill to max. Season the pork on both sides with salt and pepper, place on a tray and grill for about 6 minutes on each side (bone-in chops will take a bit longer than boneless ones), or until the meat is cooked through – cut into a thick part of the pork and make sure the raw pink flesh has turned grey.

Heat the remaining butter in a large saucepan over a medium to high heat. When hot, add the garlic and thyme leaves and cook for 2 minutes. Cut any of the large spring green leaves in half, then add all the greens to the pan with 50ml of water. Cover with a lid and let them cook like this for 6 minutes, or until the leaves are tender. Remove the lid, pour in the cream, season with salt and pepper and give everything a good stir.

Serve the mash topped with a pork chop and a good helping of creamy greens.

TIP

Cream freezes extremely well and can be added to dishes from frozen to provide a luxurious finishing touch.

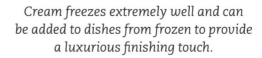

FAMILY FAVOURITES

PORK SCHNITZEL WITH POTATO SALAD

SERVES 4

Pork fillet is the cheapest fillet that you'll find in the supermarket – it's a fraction of the cost of beef, lamb or even chicken. I'm not sure why because it delivers like other fillets – it's lean and tender to eat. You won't believe how far a 500g piece of meat will go, once it's been breadcrumbed and combined with an egg and potato salad.

PREP TIME 20 MINUTES
COOKING TIME 30 MINUTES

500g pork fillet (sometimes called tenderloin), cut into 4 equal pieces
50g plain flour
3 eggs
80g breadcrumbs
a pinch of dried sage
1 lemon, zest only
750g new potatoes, scrubbed clean and halved
2 tbsp vegetable oil
3 spring onions, trimmed and finely sliced
2 tsp capers, drained and roughly chopped
2 tbsp mayonnaise
a handful of lettuce leaves, to serve

Take each piece of pork one at a time and place it on a chopping board, cut side up. Lay a piece of clingfilm over the meat and, using a meat mallet or other blunt object, bash the meat until it is about ½ cm thick – shape is not important, but try to achieve an even thinness. Season with salt and pepper, and repeat the process with the remaining pieces of pork.

Tip the flour on to a plate and crack 1 egg into a shallow dish and whisk well. Tip the breadcrumbs on to a third plate and stir in the sage and lemon zest.

Take each piece of bashed pork in turn and place first in the flour, turning so both sides are coated. Dip into the egg, turning again, and finally place and turn in the breadcrumbs so the meat is well covered.

Put a large pot of water on to boil and, when boiling, drop in the potatoes and cook for 5 minutes. Add the remaining eggs in their shells to the pot and boil for a further 9 minutes, or until the potatoes are cooked through. Drain the potatoes and eggs.

Meanwhile, heat half the oil in a large, non-stick frying pan over a medium to high heat and, when hot, gently add two pieces of pork. Fry for 3 minutes on each side, or until the pork is cooked through. Slide the cooked schnitzels from the pan and cover with a piece of tin foil to keep them warm. Repeat the process with the remaining oil and schnitzels.

Transfer the potatoes to a bowl. Peel and roughly break up the eggs straight into the bowl with the potatoes. Add the spring onions, capers and mayonnaise, along with a good pinch of both salt and pepper, and gently stir the ingredients together.

Serve the schnitzels with a large portion of warm potato salad and a few lettuce leaves on the side.

CHORIZO & BLACK OLIVE PAELLA

SERVES 4

There are so many regional variations of paella – here we're combining chorizo and prawns. Frozen prawns are often frozen at sea, as soon as they're caught, which locks in flavour and nutrition. They're not a substandard product and are convenient and cheaper than fresh. You do need a specific type of rice for this dish – bomba is the classic but the slightly cheaper arborio can also be used.

PREP TIME 10 MINUTES
COOKING TIME 45 MINUTES

---

a few strands of saffron
400ml chicken stock
1 tbsp olive oil
50g chorizo, cut into 1cm pieces
1 red onion, peeled and diced
1 celery stalk, washed and diced
350g arborio rice
½ tsp turmeric
1 tsp sweet smoked paprika
100g runner beans, or green
   beans, cut into 2cm pieces
1 x 400g tin chopped tomatoes
200g frozen prawns, defrosted
60g frozen peas
25g pitted black olives
1 lemon, cut into wedges,
   to serve
½ small bunch of fresh
   parsley, chopped

Drop the saffron into a large jug filled with hot chicken stock. Leave the liquid to infuse.

Heat the olive oil in a wide casserole over a medium to high heat and, when hot, add the chorizo, onion and celery, and sweat, stirring regularly, for 8 minutes.

Add the rice and mix in with the other ingredients. Sprinkle in the spices and add the runner beans. Continue to fry for another 2 minutes, stirring almost constantly.

Pour in the chopped tomatoes and the infused chicken stock. Bring the liquid to the boil, cover with a lid, reduce the heat and simmer for 20 minutes, or until the rice is fully cooked through and the stock has almost all been absorbed.

Remove the lid and scatter the prawns, peas and black olives over the top of the rice. Put the lid back on and cook for a further 5 minutes. Turn off the heat and leave to sit with the lid on for a final 5 minutes.

Scatter the lemon wedges and parsley over the top of the paella before serving.

CALABRIAN LASAGNE

SERVES 4

And you thought there was only one type of lasagne. Well, there are actually many recipes – this one is a bit simpler than the traditional.

PREP TIME 30 MINUTES
COOKING TIME 75 MINUTES

—

4 eggs
1 tbsp olive oil
1 onion, peeled and diced
2 cloves garlic, peeled
   and finely chopped
1 tbsp tomato puree
150g minced beef
200g minced pork
600g passata
600ml beef stock
300g lasagne pasta sheets
125g cooked ham
1 large bunch of fresh basil,
   leaves separated
200g mozzarella, sliced thinly

Bring a pan of water to the boil and cook the eggs for 9 minutes. Drain and cool under running water. Peel the eggs and then cut them roughly into ½cm slices.

Preheat the oven to 180°C/Gas 4.

Heat the oil in a large frying pan over a medium to high heat. When hot, fry the onion and garlic together for 5 minutes, or until softened.

Turn up the heat and add the tomato puree, frying it for 1 minute, before adding both the minced meats. Fry the meat for about 5 minutes, breaking it up with a wooden spoon.

Pour in the passata and the stock. Bring the liquid up to the boil, season well with salt and pepper and then take the pan off the heat.

Ladle enough of the loose meat mixture to cover the base of a baking dish. Cover with lasagne sheets and then pour more sauce on top. Add half of the ham, eggs, basil leaves and mozzarella. Lay more pasta sheets on top, pour over more sauce and add the rest of the ham, eggs and basil. Lay a final layer of pasta on top, pour over all of the remaining sauce and dot with the last of the mozzarella.

Cover the dish with tin foil and bake in the preheated oven for 50 minutes.

Remove the foil and bake for a further 10 minutes, or until lightly golden on top. Take the lasagne out of the oven and leave to rest for 5 minutes before serving.

TIP

Look closely at the prices of passata and tinned tomatoes before you buy – sometimes passata can be cheaper.

TEX MEX CHILLI SERVES 6

This is sure to be a family favourite! Add even more jalapenos if you like it hot. Store celery in tin foil – there is no build up of decomposing gases and the foil seems to help regulate its humidity.

PREP TIME 25 MINUTES
COOKING TIME 90 MINUTES

2 tbsp sunflower oil
2 onions, peeled and diced
2 celery stalks, washed, trimmed and diced
2 carrots, peeled and diced (roughly 200g)
1 tsp smoked paprika
1 tsp ground cumin
1 tbsp tomato puree
1 x 400g tin chopped tomatoes
200ml beef stock
300g minced turkey
300g minced beef
1 x 400g tin kidney beans, drained and rinsed
1 x 400g tin baked beans
150g long grain rice
60ml soured cream, to serve
1 small bunch of fresh coriander, roughly chopped
40g jalapenos, chopped

Heat half of the oil in a large casserole dish over a medium to high heat and, when hot, add the onions, celery and carrots, and cook, stirring regularly, for 6 minutes, or until all the vegetables have started to soften.

Sprinkle in the paprika and cumin, and continue to stir and fry for 30 seconds. Add the tomato puree and cook for another minute, or until the puree turns a shade darker. Stir in the tomatoes and stock and bring the whole lot slowly to a simmer.

Heat the remaining oil in a separate frying pan over a high heat. When the oil is smoking hot, add both the minced meats and leave them to fry hard for 1 minute, before breaking up with a spoon. When the meat is browned all over, tip the entire contents of the frying pan into the large casserole with the cooking vegetables.

Bring the mixture to the boil, then place a cocked lid on top and reduce the heat to a gentle simmer. Cook the chilli like this for about 1 hour.

Tip in the kidney beans and baked beans and continue to cook, this time uncovered, for a further 15 minutes.

Whilst the chilli is finishing off, cook the rice according to packet instructions.

Serve the chilli on top of steaming rice with a dollop of soured cream, a sprinkling of coriander and a scattering of jalapenos, for those who love a bit of heat.

TIP

Soured cream often comes in annoyingly large containers. Don't let the remnants go off in the fridge; instead use the cream in bread recipes or cheesecakes.

BEEF BOURGUIGNON

SERVES 4-6

Sounds fancy, but it's really just a beef stew loaded with wine and some bacon for flavour. Beef shin is arguably the best cut of meat for a stew; the fact that it is also one of the cheapest cuts of beef is a huge bonus. Dishes like this are brilliant served with mash or bread – warming, filling and filled with good-quality protein. Browning the meat is one of the most important parts of this recipe. Colour equals flavour.

PREP TIME 30 MINUTES
COOKING TIME 120 MINUTES

1 tbsp vegetable oil
600g beef shin, cut into large
　3–4cm chunks
1 onion, peeled and diced
3 rashers smoked streaky bacon,
　cut into 1cm strips
300g carrots, peeled and diced
125g button mushrooms, roughly
　chopped into quarters
1 tbsp tomato puree
1 sprig of fresh thyme
1 bay leaf
175ml red wine
200ml beef stock,
　made with 1 cube
500g potatoes, peeled and
　cut into large 3cm chunks
1 tbsp butter
½ small bunch of fresh parsley,
　roughly chopped
loaf of bread, to serve

Heat half the oil in a large casserole over a medium to high heat and, when hot, add half the meat and brown all over. Remove to a plate and add the rest of the beef to brown. Once this is done, set aside with the other meat.

Pour the remaining oil into the casserole and add the onion, bacon, carrots and mushrooms, and fry, stirring regularly, for 8 minutes. Turn down the heat a little if you think the ingredients are burning on the base.

Add the tomato puree, thyme sprig and bay leaf, and stir them into the other ingredients.

Tip the browned meat back into the casserole and pour in the wine. Bring the liquid up to a boil and simmer until it has reduced by about half.

Pour in the stock, bring back to a simmer and cook with a cocked lid for about 1 hour 30 minutes, or until the meat is meltingly tender.

When the beef has about 30 minutes left to cook, boil the potatoes in a large saucepan of water for about 20 minutes, or until they are very tender. Drain thoroughly, tip back into their pan, add the butter and a good pinch of salt, and mash until you reach a smooth texture.

Sprinkle the stew with the parsley and serve with piles of mash and thick slices of bread.

BEEF STEW WITH DUMPLINGS

SERVES 4

Don't assume that simply picking up a pack of stewing beef is how to shop for a stew! The fact is that the meat in those packs is often just the trimmings from more expensive cuts and is not suited to stewing – you also pay for the packaging. Head to the butcher's counter instead and ask for cuts like oxtail, shin or cheek, which are cheap and perfect for a low and slow cook.

PREP TIME 15 MINUTES
COOKING TIME 135 MINUTES

—

2 tbsp sunflower oil
2 onions, peeled and diced
2 celery stalks, washed
    and diced
100g carrots, peeled, trimmed
    and diced
200g potatoes, scrubbed
    clean and diced
2 bay leaves
1 star anise
7cm orange peel
2 tbsp tomato puree
500ml beef stock
700g beef shin, cut roughly
    into 3cm chunks
250g self-raising flour
1 heaped tsp mustard powder
60g butter, diced

Heat half the oil in a large, ovenproof casserole dish over a medium heat. When hot, add the onions, celery, carrots and potatoes. Fry for about 8 minutes, until they are nicely softened, stirring regularly.

Add the bay leaf, star anise, orange peel and tomato puree and fry for another 2 minutes, stirring occasionally.

Pour in the stock and slowly bring to a simmer.

Meanwhile, season the beef all over with salt and pepper and pour half the remaining oil into a large frying pan over a high heat. When the oil is smoking hot, carefully lay half the beef in the frying pan and cook until dark golden brown all over. Tip into the casserole dish and repeat the browning process with the remaining oil and beef. When this second batch is ready, tip it in as well.

Place a cocked lid on top of the dish and simmer the stew for about 90 minutes, or until the meat is very tender.

Preheat the oven to 180°C/Gas 4.

Tip the flour and mustard into a large bowl, add a good pinch of both salt and pepper, and then rub the butter into the flour with your fingers, until the mixture resembles breadcrumbs. Pour in 50ml of water and give the ingredients a good stir. It will start to come together but you will need to add a little more water until it reaches a firm but not dry texture that you can handle easily.

Roll the mixture into 8 balls, roughly the size of a walnut, and drop them directly into the stew, leaving a good amount of space between each dumpling.

Replace the lid, bring the stew slowly back up to the boil and then bake in the preheated oven for 15 minutes.

Carefully remove the casserole from the oven, take off the lid and spoon a little of the stew gravy over the top of the dumplings. Return the casserole to the oven and bake for a further 15 minutes, by which time the dumplings will have puffed up and developed a very satisfying golden top.

Serve up and enjoy.

TIP

When storing carrots and courgettes, you should wrap them in kitchen roll and then put them in plastic bags or tin foil before placing in the fridge – this stops condensation from softening the veg and stops mould forming, too, making them last longer.

BONUS BOLOGNAISE

SERVES 8

Here's a meal that fills the tummy and comforts the soul. It's also a meal that your wallet will like – it's great value for money! Mixing two types of minced meat is not only a good way to save money, as you pad out expensive beef with slightly cheaper pork, but it's also a very traditionally Italian way to cook. The quantities given here will produce enough bolognaise for two meals for four people – see the tip below for ideas about how to use the leftovers.

PREP TIME 15 MINUTES
COOKING TIME 90 MINUTES

40ml vegetable oil
2 onions, peeled and diced
100g carrot, peeled and diced
1 celery stalk, washed and diced
2 cloves garlic, peeled
   and minced
1 bay leaf
1 sprig of fresh thyme
1 tbsp tomato puree
1 x 400g tin chopped tomatoes
400ml beef stock
300g minced beef
400g minced pork
1 x 400g tin borlotti beans,
   drained and rinsed
375g spaghetti
a glug of olive oil

Heat half the oil in a large casserole dish over a medium to high heat. When hot, fry the onions, carrot and celery for 5 minutes, or until they just begin to soften. Add the garlic, bay leaf and thyme and fry for a further 2 minutes. Add the tomato puree and continue to stir and fry for another minute. Add the tomatoes and stock and bring slowly up to a simmer.

Whilst the sauce is coming up to the boil, heat half the remaining oil in a large frying pan over a high heat. When smoking hot, add the beef mince and fry, without stirring, for 45 seconds. Start to break up the mince and continue frying until it is totally broken up and browned in a few areas. Tip into the sauce.

Heat the remaining oil in the same pan over a high heat. When smoking hot, add the pork mince and fry, without stirring, for 90 seconds. Start to break up the mince and continue to fry until broken up and brown in a few areas. Add to the sauce.

Place a cocked lid on the casserole dish and simmer the bolognaise for 1 hour, stirring every now and then so that it doesn't burn on the base. After 1 hour, add the beans and continue to cook for 15 minutes, until the meat is tender and the sauce thickened.

Once the beans have been added, bring a large pot of water to the boil and cook the spaghetti according to the packet instructions.

Drain, season with a glug of olive oil, salt and pepper, and serve topped with generous amounts of bolognaise.

TIP

Serve up half this bolognaise with spaghetti and use the other half to make Classic Lasagne (page 114) or Bolognaise Pasties (page 145).

CLASSIC LASAGNE SERVES 4

The comfort food other comfort foods turn to when they've had a bad day, lasagne is the gastronomic version of a hug from your mum. The good news is that once the bolognaise part of the dish is sorted it becomes a very easy meal to prepare. Infusing milk is a wonderful way to turn a decent lasagne into a great one, so be sure to keep any off cuts of onion and celery, which can be used to flavour your white sauce.

PREP TIME 25 MINUTES
COOKING TIME 40 MINUTES
——
500ml milk
outer layer of 1 onion (30g)
off cuts of celery
1 bay leaf
70g butter
70g plain flour
300g lasagne pasta sheets
700g Bonus Bolognaise
   (page 113)
50g Parmesan, grated
salad, to serve

Preheat the oven to 180°C/Gas 4.

Pour the milk into a saucepan and add the onion, celery and bay leaf. Bring the milk to the boil and simmer for 30 seconds. Turn off the heat and leave to sit and infuse for 20 minutes. Strain the milk.

Heat the butter in a clean saucepan and, when melted, stir in the flour. Cook, stirring almost constantly, for 2 minutes and then take off the heat and stir in one third of the infused milk until it is totally absorbed. Put the pan back on the heat and add the remaining milk, a little at a time, stirring in between additions to make sure you don't get any lumps. When you have a smooth, slightly glossy sauce, bring it up to the boil and simmer for 1 minute, stirring almost constantly, and then turn off the heat.

Spoon a little of the white sauce into the base of a baking dish (23 x 15cm), spreading it out to cover the base evenly. Lay a few lasagne sheets (normally about 3) on the white sauce and then spread half of the bolognaise over the pasta. Drizzle a little more of the white sauce on top of the bolognaise and then cover with a few more sheets of pasta. Spread over the remainder of the mince, drizzle with a little white sauce and then lay your final sheets of pasta on top.

Pour over the remaining white sauce, which should cover the surface of the lasagne, and then sprinkle with the Parmesan. Bake in the preheated oven for 35–40 minutes, or until the lasagne is bubbling hot, golden on top and the pasta is fully cooked through.

Remove from the oven and leave to sit for 5 minutes before serving with a little salad on the side.

LEFTOVERS &
STORE CUPBOARD

TEAR & SHARE BREAD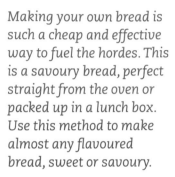

Making your own bread is such a cheap and effective way to fuel the hordes. This is a savoury bread, perfect straight from the oven or packed up in a lunch box. Use this method to make almost any flavoured bread, sweet or savoury.

PREP TIME 15 MINUTES,
PLUS 120 MINUTES PROVING
COOKING TIME 50 MINUTES
—

1 tbsp vegetable oil
3 red onions, peeled
   and finely sliced
1 sprig of thyme
1 tbsp balsamic vinegar
1 tsp brown sugar
½ x 7g packet fast action yeast
650g strong bread flour, plus
   a little extra for dusting
100g hard mozzarella, chopped
   roughly into 2cm pieces
100g ham
salad, to serve

Heat the oil in a large frying pan over a medium heat and, when hot, add the onions. Cook for about 20 minutes, turning them every now and then, until they are meltingly tender and lightly browned.

Turn the heat up to maximum and add the thyme, vinegar and sugar. Fry, stirring constantly, for 3 minutes, and then tip the mixture on to a tray and leave to cool completely.

Place the yeast in a large jug and add 300ml of warm water. Mix the yeast into the water as well as you can.

Tip the flour into a large bowl and make a small indent in the middle. Gradually stir the warm yeast water into the flour and, when it has all been incorporated, start kneading. When the dough is starting to come together, tip on to a lightly floured surface and knead for 5 minutes. Tip the dough into a clean bowl, cover with clingfilm and leave to prove for about 90 minutes.

Tip the dough, which should have doubled in size, on to a floured surface and bash it, in order to knock out the air. Using a rolling pin, roll out to a rough rectangle 40 x 20cm.

Spread the cooled onion mix all over the bread and then scatter the mozzarella over the top. Tear up the ham and add this, too. Starting at the long end closest to you, roll the dough into a big sausage shape, tucking in as you go. Cut into 8 equal pieces.

Place the pieces of dough, cut side up, close to each other on a baking or roasting tray, cover loosely with clingfilm and leave to prove for a further 30 minutes.

Preheat the oven to 220°C/Gas 7.

Uncover the bread and bake in the preheated oven for about 40 minutes, or until completely cooked through.

Remove from the oven, leave to cool for 10 minutes on the tray, then transfer to a board and start to tear and share.

SWEET POTATO HASH

This is a great way to use up odds and ends of vegetables kicking around in the fridge. The microwave – so often maligned – can be key to speedy suppers. There is chorizo in this recipe – a little goes a long way and it keeps in the fridge for a long time.

PREP TIME 10 MINUTES
COOKING TIME 15 MINUTES

———

3 medium sweet potatoes
  (about 500g), scrubbed clean
1 tbsp olive oil
75g chorizo, diced
1 red onion, peeled and diced
1 broccoli head, florets only,
  chopped into small pieces
½ red pepper, de-seeded
  and diced
sprinkling of fajita mix
a large handful of spinach
  (about 75g)
4 eggs
4 chunky slices of bread,
  to serve

Prick the sweet potatoes all over with a fork then zap in the microwave for 4 minutes. Rest them for 2 minutes and then zap for a further 4 minutes. Leave the potatoes to rest and cool. When the sweet potato is cool enough to handle, peel them and cut into cubes.

Heat the oil in a large frying pan over a medium to high heat and chuck in the chorizo, onion, broccoli and red pepper and fry for 3 minutes. Crank up the heat to maximum and add the sweet potato and a sprinkling of the fajita mix. Fry together for about 5 minutes and then stir through the spinach until it's wilted.

Make 4 indentations in the mix and crack an egg into each one. Cover the pan with a lid and cook for about 5 minutes, or until the egg whites are cooked but the yolks are still a little runny.

Serve with the bread.

TIP

*Don't throw your broccoli stalk away –
use it in a soup (page 124).*

CHICKEN STOCK

MAKES 1·5 LITRES

The old adage claimed that from one roast chicken you could derive enough meals to last an entire week. Although this may be true, I'm not convinced we really want to go that far. Having said that, to throw away the carcass and all the meaty pickings after a roast is a crime. The following recipes are designed to show you how to make the most of your roast bird.

PREP TIME 10 MINUTES
COOKING TIME 120 MINUTES

—

1 chicken carcass, skin, bones, everything
1 onion, peeled and roughly chopped
3 sprigs of fresh thyme
1 bay leaf
2 celery stalks, washed and roughly chopped
100g carrots, peeled and roughly chopped

Place all the ingredients in a large saucepan and cover with water. Bring the liquid to the boil, skimming any scum off as it rises to the surface.

Reduce the heat to a simmer and cook for 2 hours.

Strain the stock and leave to cool to room temperature before freezing or refrigerating.

TIP

Chicken stock freezes brilliantly and can be added from frozen to soups and sauces. Be sure to portion it up before freezing, though.

APPLE, PARSNIP & CELERIAC SOUP WITH CHILLI CROUTONS

SERVES 4

The key to this dish is caramelising all the vegetables in the pan before adding any liquids. All the vegetables have a delicious, deep, slightly sweet flavour that comes out with frying, so don't skip this step or you'll end up with a very ordinary soup. The crumbs at the bottom of your bread bag, the ones that nobody ever seems to want, make delicious croutons.

PREP TIME 20 MINUTES
COOKING TIME 30 MINUTES

2 tbsp vegetable oil
2 onions, peeled and diced
700g celeriac, scrubbed clean and cut into 3cm chunks
300g parsnips, scrubbed clean and cut into 3cm chunks
125g apples, peeled, cored and roughly chopped
250g potatoes, scrubbed clean and roughly chopped into 3cm chunks
2 tsp garam masala
1 litre chicken stock
250g bread, from breadcrumbs to crusts, broken into croutons
1 clove garlic, peeled and finely chopped
1 red chilli, trimmed and cut into thin slices

Heat half the oil in a large saucepan over a medium to high heat and, once hot, add the onions and cook, stirring every now and then, for 5 minutes.

Add the celeriac, parsnips, apples and potatoes and cook for a further 8–10 minutes, stirring every now and again. You are looking to colour some of the vegetables in places, so don't be afraid to leave the pan for a couple of minutes between each stir.

Crank up the heat to maximum and sprinkle in the garam masala, stirring to coat all the ingredients lightly. Continue to stir and fry for a further 1 minute.

Pour in the stock and bring to a boil. Simmer for about 20 minutes, or until all the ingredients are very soft.

Whilst the soup is simmering, heat half the remaining oil in a large frying pan over a medium to high heat. When it is hot, add half the bread to the pan and fry for about 1 minute, turning regularly to avoid burning.

Stir in half the garlic and chilli and fry for a minute before removing the croutons to a plate. Repeat with the remaining oil, bread, garlic and chilli.

When you're happy that the vegetables are very soft, turn off the heat and blitz the ingredients until smooth using a blender.

Serve each bowl of soup topped with a good amount of spiced croutons.

TIP

Don't throw bruised apples away: stew them up to make apple sauce to serve with yoghurt or a roast.

OFF CUT VEG SOUP

SERVES 4

Why do people buy broccoli and throw the stalk away? This soup utilises the normally discarded parts of vegetables to make a great soup. Add a poached egg for a more substantial meal. Adding the spinach right at the end gives the soup a vibrant green colour and also safeguards as many of the nutrients as possible. Tofu is cheaper than meat, but contains a good amount of protein, which is the stuff that makes you feel full for longer. People say they don't like it, but nobody will even know it's in this soup.

PREP TIME 10 MINUTES
COOKING TIME 20 MINUTES

3 tbsp vegetable oil
green tops of a leek or spring
    onions, roughly chopped
    (about 80g)
1 potato (about 200g), scrubbed
    clean and diced
leaves and stem from 1
    cauliflower, roughly chopped
    (about 200g)
stalk from 1 head of broccoli,
    roughly diced (about 100g)
1 litre vegetable or chicken stock
100g silken tofu
a large handful of spinach
    (about 50g)
4 slices of stale bread
4 eggs

Heat 1 tablespoon of the oil in a saucepan and add the leek or spring onions, potato, cauliflower leaves and broccoli stalk and fry for about 2 minutes.

Pour in the stock and simmer for 15–20 minutes, or until soft. Add the tofu for the last 3–4 minutes of cooking. Blitz the ingredients, adding the spinach as you do, until smooth. Season with salt and pepper to taste.

Whilst the soup is cooking, heat the rest of the oil in a large frying pan. Roughly break up the bread in your hands into small pieces and then fry until golden brown. Remove the crumbs to a clean piece of kitchen roll and leave to cool.

Crack the eggs into a large pot of boiling water and reduce the heat right down so the water is barely bubbling. Cook the eggs like this for 4–5 minutes for a soft yolk.

Serve the soup in bowls with a poached egg on the top of each one and then scatter with the fried crumbs.

TIP

Blitz leftover cooked broccoli with milk to make a creamy sauce for chicken or fish.

RISOTTO ALLA MILANESE

What, saffron, in a £5 recipe, surely not? Yes, well, the thing about saffron is that, although it's expensive, a little goes a very long way. This risotto is the food of Italian royalty, classically served with stewed veal leg. We've gone for a more humble approach, replacing hard-to-find bone marrow with the store cupboard staples butter and Bovril. It might not be an exact gastro replica, but it definitely is tasty.

PREP TIME 10 MINUTES
COOKING TIME 40 MINUTES
—

1.2 litres chicken stock
a few strands of saffron
85g butter
2 onions, peeled and diced
500g risotto rice
20g Bovril
40g Parmesan, grated
½ small bunch of fresh
    parsley, stalks and all,
    finely chopped

Bring the stock up to the boil over a high heat and, when hot, turn off the hob and add the saffron. Leave to infuse in the hot stock for 10 minutes.

Heat 35g of the butter in a large saucepan over a medium to high heat and, when melted and bubbling, slide in the onion and fry, stirring regularly, for 6–7 minutes, or until softened.

Stir in the rice and fry with the onions for 1 minute, stirring almost constantly. Stir in a ladleful of stock, which will bubble up and slowly be absorbed by the rice. When there is almost no stock left in the pan, pour in a second ladleful. Repeat the process until all of the stock is used up, the rice is cooked through and has become creamy.

Reduce the heat to medium low and stir in the remaining butter, Bovril and Parmesan. Place a lid on your pan and leave for 5 minutes.

After 5 minutes stir in the parsley, season with salt and pepper and serve.

TIP

Store cheese in wax paper to keep it fresh for longer.

MUSHROOM RISOTTO

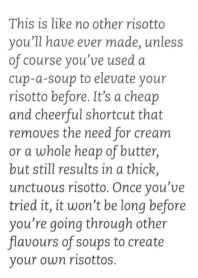

SERVES 4

This is like no other risotto you'll have ever made, unless of course you've used a cup-a-soup to elevate your risotto before. It's a cheap and cheerful shortcut that removes the need for cream or a whole heap of butter, but still results in a thick, unctuous risotto. Once you've tried it, it won't be long before you're going through other flavours of soups to create your own risottos.

PREP TIME 10 MINUTES
COOKING TIME 40 MINUTES

—

1.25 litres chicken stock
1 heaped tbsp butter
1 tbsp olive oil
1 onion, peeled and diced
200g mushrooms, brushed clean and roughly chopped into quarters
300g risotto rice
100ml white wine
2 x sachets Cream of Mushroom Soup
30g Parmesan, grated
½ small bunch of fresh parsley, chopped

Pour the stock into a saucepan, bring to the boil and then turn off the heat.

Heat the butter and oil together in a large saucepan over a medium heat. When melted and bubbling, add the onion and cook for 5–6 minutes, or until just softening and translucent.

Turn up the heat to maximum and add the mushrooms, frying them until lightly brown.

Stir in the rice and continue to fry all the ingredients together for 2 minutes, stirring almost constantly.

Pour in the wine and let it bubble up and pretty much evaporate, then add a ladleful of hot stock. Reduce the heat a little and stir the rice and stock together until the stock has been absorbed and then add a second ladleful. Continue to add stock and stir until it is all used up and the rice is just cooked through – it should be tender to eat, whilst still retaining a slight bite.

Now for the magic – reduce the heat to minimum and stir in the sachets of soup and the Parmesan. The risotto should become thick and creamy. Add a little more stock, or hot water, if needed.

Stir through the parsley, season well with salt and pepper and serve.

TIP

Keep your olive oil out of the sun to make it last longer.

PASTA GENOVESE

SERVES 4

This is a classic Italian dish that relies on the heavenly combination of double carbs. In this pasta dish the potatoes become the sauce. Because there is no meat, you can spend a bit more on the flavoursome Parmesan which, with the help of some basil, transforms this dish from peasant mainstay to brilliantly economic and tasty family favourite.

PREP TIME 10 MINUTES
COOKING TIME 30 MINUTES

- 400g potatoes, peeled and roughly cut into 3cm chunks
- 400g spaghetti
- 200g fine green beans, topped and tailed
- 125g fresh basil, stalks and all, plus extra for garnish
- 125g Parmesan, plus extra grated for garnish
- 1 clove garlic
- 75ml olive oil

Bring a large pan of water to the boil over a high heat and carefully drop in the potatoes. Cook for about 15 minutes, or until cooked through.

Add the spaghetti and cook for a further 10 minutes (this is based on the pasta taking 12 minutes to cook).

Add the beans to the same pot and cook for a further 2 minutes.

Just before draining the cooked ingredients, scoop out half a mugful of the starch-rich cooking liquid (about 125ml) and keep to one side. Drain the ingredients through a colander and then tip back into the large pot they were cooked in.

While the pasta is cooking, place all the remaining ingredients in a food processor and blitz until smooth.

Tip the instant pesto over the cooked pasta, potatoes and beans, pour in the cooking liquor, season well with salt and pepper and give everything a good stir. The potatoes will totally break up and combine with the cooking liquid and pesto to create a silky smooth sauce.

Garnish with some basil leaves and grated Parmesan and serve your traditional Italian feast.

TIP

Store potatoes with apples – the ethylene in the apples will keep the potatoes from sprouting.

SALMON FISHCAKES WITH EASY LEMON HOLLANDAISE

SERVES 4

Over the years fresh salmon has been steadily rising in price to a point where it can't really be considered an affordable protein source. The good news is that tinned salmon continues to be cheap. You'll still benefit not only from the healthy fats associated with salmon, but also from the low, low price.

PREP TIME 25 MINUTES
COOKING TIME 30 MINUTES

—

400g potatoes, peeled and
    cut into 3cm chunks
1 x 270g tin salmon, drained
1 tbsp Dijon mustard
60g spring onions, finely sliced
3 eggs
½ small bunch of fresh dill,
    finely chopped, stalks and all
½ small bunch of fresh parsley,
    finely chopped, stalks and all
90g breadcrumbs
50g plain flour
25ml lemon juice
100g butter, melted
100ml vegetable oil
a little baby spinach, to serve

Boil the potatoes in a large pot of salted water until very tender. Drain through a colander, giving them a good shake to remove as much excess liquid as possible.

Tip the potatoes into a large bowl and then fork in the salmon, breaking it up into small pieces. Add half the mustard, the spring onions, 1 egg and both the dill and parsley, along with a generous pinch of salt and pepper. Thoroughly mix the ingredients together and then roughly divide into 4.

Using wet hands, take each quarter of mix and shape into a disc about 3cm thick.

Spread the breadcrumbs on a plate and tip the flour on to a second plate.

Separate 2 eggs, dropping the yolks into a big bowl and the whites on to a third plate. Give the whites a little whisk with a fork to become frothy.

Take each fishcake in turn and dip into the flour, giving it a little pat to remove any excess. Dunk the floured fishcake into the egg whites, turning to ensure total coverage. Finally drop it into the breadcrumbs and turn to cover totally. Repeat the process with the remaining fishcakes. Put the breadcrumbed fishcakes into the fridge to firm up for a few minutes.

Whilst the fishcakes are in the fridge, bring a medium saucepan of water up to the boil.

Whisk the lemon juice and remaining mustard into the two saved egg yolks. Place the bowl on top of the saucepan of boiling water, making sure the base of the bowl doesn't come into contact with the simmering water. Whisk the ingredients over the heat for 2 minutes, by which time the mix should increase in volume, turn paler in colour and become thicker. If it hasn't then continue to whisk.

Begin drizzling in the melted butter, whisking pretty much continuously. Start slowly with the butter, ensuring it emulsifies before adding any more. Continue until all of the butter has been incorporated and you have a thick sauce. Taste and season with salt and pepper, if needed. Turn the heat off under the pan, but leave the sauce on top to keep warm.

Pour the oil into a large frying pan over a medium to high heat. When hot, place the fishcakes in the oil and shallow fry for 3 minutes on each side, or until the outside is golden and crisp and the inside is piping hot.

Serve the fishcakes with the spinach and lashings of hollandaise sauce.

TIP

Leftover mashed potato is great for making fishcakes.

TUNA & SWEETCORN FRITTERS SERVES 4

This is a recipe that will take you right back to childhood with the familiar flavour of tuna and sweetcorn. It might not be the most remarkable dish in the book, but it is one of the tastiest.

PREP TIME 5 MINUTES
COOKING TIME 10 MINUTES

---

2 x 120g tins tuna
1 x 140g tin sweetcorn
2 tbsp plain flour
1 egg yolk
1 spring onion, thinly sliced
a little oil, to fry
chilli sauce, to serve
soy sauce, to serve

Flake the tuna into a bowl, drain the sweetcorn and mix the two together.

Add the flour, egg yolk and spring onion and mix together well. Gradually add a little water until you have a thick batter.

Heat a little oil in a frying pan over a medium heat. When hot, spoon large tablespoons of the mix into the pan and make small fritters. Fry for about 2 minutes on each side, until browned and cooked through.

Serve with some chilli or soy sauce.

TIP

Don't throw the egg white away – freeze it for another day.

SARDINE & BROCCOLI LINGUINI  SERVES 4

We all know we should eat more oily fish for the omega 3 and healthy fats that help our brains and general health in all sorts of wonderful ways. Well, forget about the health benefits for a moment and instead concentrate on taste and budget. Not only are sardines incredibly cheap, they are also very tasty and, when bought in a tin, they are ready to pull from the cupboard at any time. So, go ahead and make this dish knowing that it is good for mind, body, soul, tastebuds and bank balance.

PREP TIME 5 MINUTES
COOKING TIME 20 MINUTES

—

250g linguini
1 head of broccoli, florets only
4 tbsp olive oil
3 cloves garlic, bashed
1 red onion, peeled and diced
2 x 120g tins sardines in oil
3 slices of stale bread, grated
   to breadcrumbs
½ lemon, juice only
1 small bunch of fresh
   parsley, roughly chopped

Bring a large pan of salted water to the boil and, when bubbling, drop in the linguini and cook according to packet instructions. Two minutes before the end of the cooking time, drop in the broccoli and then drain the whole lot together.

Whilst the pasta is cooking, heat half the oil in a large frying pan over a medium to high heat and, when hot, add the garlic and onion and fry, stirring regularly, for 4 minutes, or until soft.

Drain the sardines and roughly chunk them up into the frying pan. Don't overcook, just warm them through and then turn off the heat.

Heat the remaining oil in a separate large frying pan over a high heat and, when almost smoking, tip in the breadcrumbs and fry until golden and crisp. Remove to a clean piece of kitchen roll with a slotted spoon.

Put the heat back on under the sardine sauce and add the cooked linguini and broccoli. Toss the whole lot together and season with salt, pepper and lemon juice.

Finish by stirring through the parsley and topping with the crispy breadcrumbs.

TIP

Use cooking tongs to help you get all the juice out of a lemon – put the lemon half inside the tongs and squeeze with both hands.

CHICKEN & TARRAGON PASTA BAKE

SERVES 4

*Pasta bake is here to stay –
it's such an amazing way to
fill up a hungry family and
is seriously cheap. Putting
breadcrumbs on top makes it
both more filling and gives the
dish a different texture. Why
does everybody think broccoli
stalks are inedible? They taste
just like broccoli florets!*

PREP TIME 30 MINUTES
COOKING TIME 30 MINUTES

—

350g penne pasta
175g broccoli, florets separated,
   and stalk chopped into
   2cm chunks
300g Chicken and Leek Pie
   filling (see 71), or alternative
   chicken sauce (see Tip below)
1 small bunch of fresh tarragon,
   finely chopped
50g fresh white breadcrumbs
2 sprigs of fresh thyme,
   leaves only

Preheat the oven to 200°C/Gas 6.

Boil the pasta according to the packet instructions. Two
minutes before the end of the cooking time, drop in the
broccoli florets and pieces of stalk and continue to cook
with the pasta. Just before draining, scoop out half a
mugful of the starchy cooking liquid. Drain the pasta
and broccoli through a colander and run under cold
water to cool. Leave in the colander to cool completely.

Tip the pie filling into a big bowl and add the reserved
pasta water and the tarragon. Tip in the pasta and
broccoli and give the whole lot a good mix.

Spoon into a baking dish, sprinkle over the
breadcrumbs and thyme, and bake in the preheated
oven for 30 minutes, or until the mix is bubbling
and the top has turned golden and crisp.

TIP

*If you don't have any leftover Chicken and Leek
Pie filling then: Heat 50g butter over a medium
to high heat until bubbling and melted. Add 1 finely
chopped leek and ½ finely chopped onion. Sweat the
ingredients for 5 minutes and then stir in 40g flour.
Cook this mix, stirring almost constantly, for
2 minutes and then gradually add 350–400ml
chicken stock until you reach a smooth, thick sauce.
If you have any leftover cooked chicken then
stir this through the sauce.*

LEFTOVER CHICKEN PIE CROQUETTES

SERVES 4

With a bit of mash, the pie filling lives again! And this salsa will breathe life into almost any dish.

PREP TIME 30 MINUTES
COOKING TIME 20 MINUTES

—

400g potatoes, peeled and cut into 3cm chunks
300g cooled Chicken and Leek Pie filling (page 71), or cooled alternative chicken sauce (see Tip on facing page)
1 small bunch of fresh tarragon, finely chopped
40g plain flour
2 eggs
80g breadcrumbs
1 red onion, peeled and diced
2 tbsp red wine vinegar
2 large tomatoes, roughly chopped into large chunks
1 red chilli, de-seeded and finely chopped
150ml vegetable oil
1 iceberg lettuce, shredded

Boil the potatoes until very tender, then drain thoroughly through a colander. Tip the cooked potatoes back into the pan, mash and then leave to cool.

Mix the cooled potato with the leftover pie filling and tarragon, seasoning with a little salt and pepper. Shape into 8 croquette shapes and place in the fridge to firm.

Tip the flour on to a plate, crack the eggs into a shallow bowl and beat them together, and tip the breadcrumbs on to a third plate. Take each of the croquettes, one at a time, and firstly dip in the flour, then dip in the egg and finally roll in the crumbs. Repeat the process with the remaining croquettes. Leave to one side whilst you make the salsa.

Tip the onion into a bowl and pour over the vinegar. Leave to sit for 10 minutes and then add the tomatoes and chilli, mix well and leave to one side.

Pour the oil into a high-sided frying pan over a medium to high heat and, when hot, carefully add the croquettes. Cook until golden brown all over. Remove to a clean piece of kitchen roll to dab off any excess oil.

Serve the croquettes topped with the salsa and a large handful of lettuce.

TIP

Potato skins fry up wonderfully into homemade chips, so make sure not to toss them in the bin.

CHICKEN & TARRAGON RISOTTO

Everybody should stock risotto rice: it brings almost instant luxury to any situation. Tarragon is a much underused herb – harness the flavour and you will become addicted. Any leftover risotto can be tipped into a shallow baking tray lined with clingfilm, left to set overnight then cut up into chunks and fried as little risotto cakes to have with a poached egg.

PREP TIME 15 MINUTES
COOKING TIME 35 MINUTES

800ml–1 litre chicken stock, made with 2 stock cubes
1 tbsp olive oil
1 tbsp butter
1 onion, peeled and diced
275g risotto rice
100g frozen spinach
300g leftover Chicken and Leek Pie filling (page 71), or alternative chicken sauce (see Tip on page 136)
½ small bunch of fresh tarragon, finely chopped
a few drops of truffle oil (optional)

Pour the stock into a saucepan, bring to the boil and then turn off the heat.

Heat the olive oil and butter in a large, high-sided frying pan over a medium to high heat. When the butter has melted into the oil and is bubbling, add the onion and fry for 8 minutes, or until it has softened and is translucent.

Add the rice and stir into the mix, ensuring it is nicely slicked with the oil.

Pour in a ladleful of the hot stock, stirring it into the rice. When that ladleful has been absorbed, add a second. Continue to cook, stir and add ladlefuls of stock to the rice until the stock is used up and the rice is tender.

Stir in the spinach and let it melt into the risotto. Bring the mix back up to the boil.

Finally, add the leftover chicken pie mix, stirring it in. Bring to the boil one last time and then take off the heat. Stir through the tarragon (reserving a little to garnish, if you like).

Serve with the truffle oil drizzled over the top.

SPICED SPINACH & RICOTTA CANNELLONI

SERVES 4-6

Such a satisfying dish to make and one that the whole family will enjoy. You could stuff anything into the cannelloni tubes, from simple vegetarian fillings, like spinach and ricotta, to leftover ratatouille.

PREP TIME 20 MINUTES
COOKING TIME 45 MINUTES

200g baby spinach
300g Rich Bean Stew (page 98),
  or a vegetarian alternative
  (see Tip below)
350g ricotta cheese
grating of nutmeg
250g cannelloni tubes
  (roughly 18)
1 tbsp tomato puree
2 cloves garlic, peeled
  and minced
2 x 400g tins chopped tomatoes
½ small bunch of fresh basil
100g mozzarella, torn into
  small pieces

Preheat the oven to 190°C/Gas 5. Put a kettle on to boil.

Tip the spinach into a colander and pour boiling water over to wilt it. Run cold water over the wilted spinach and, when you're certain it is cool enough to handle, give it a good squeeze to remove as much liquid as possible.

Put the spinach into a bowl and add the Rich Bean Stew, ricotta and nutmeg, along with a good pinch of salt and pepper. Stir until well combined. Stuff the mixture into the pasta tubes – don't worry if there is some mix left over: it can be added to the sauce later.

Mix together the tomato puree, garlic and tomatoes, along with a good pinch of both salt and pepper. Tip this sauce into the base of a baking dish and arrange the filled pasta tubes in a single layer on top – the sauce should almost cover the tubes. Dot with any leftover filling.

Tear half of the basil and scatter over the top. Dot with the mozzarella, cover with tin foil and bake in the preheated oven for 30 minutes.

After 30 minutes, remove the foil and continue to bake for a further 15 minutes, or until the pasta is fully cooked through and the cheese has melted and turned golden brown in spots.

Garnish with the remaining basil and serve.

TIP

If you don't have any leftover Rich Bean Stew then try making the classic spinach and ricotta cannelloni. Simply increase the amount of spinach to 600g and ricotta to 600g. Finish by grating in 50g Parmesan. This also makes for a delicious vegetarian alternative.

LEFTOVERS & STORE CUPBOARD

BACON & EGG FRIED RICE

 SERVES 4

Fried rice is a brilliant way of using up bits and bobs from your fridge, be it nuggets of cooked meat or a bit of carrot that's been lingering in the drawer. Just be sure that anything raw goes in before the rice and anything cooked goes in after. Day old rice is best – make sure it has cooled to room temperature and is covered before going into the fridge.

PREP TIME 15 MINUTES
COOKING TIME 10 MINUTES
—

2 tbsp vegetable oil
3 spring onions, finely sliced
3 cloves garlic, peeled and
    finely chopped
100g carrots, scrubbed clean
    and cut into 1cm dice
125g courgettes, topped and
    tailed and cut into 1cm dice
6 rashers smoked streaky
    bacon, cut into 1cm slices
60g frozen peas
500g cooked rice, cold
4 eggs
2 tbsp light soy sauce
2 tsp sesame oil
1 red chilli, finely sliced,
    to serve

Heat half the vegetable oil in a large frying pan or wok over a high heat. Add the spring onions to the pan, along with the garlic, carrots, courgettes and bacon. Stir-fry over the high heat for 2 minutes.

Add the peas to the pan and toss with the other ingredients. Fry for another minute, or until the dull, frozen appearance of the peas has gone.

Drop in the cooked rice, breaking it up with a wooden spoon. Pour in about 2 tablespoons of water, which will steam up and help to heat the rice through. Reduce the heat to medium and continue to stir-fry everything together until the rice is fully heated through.

Heat the remaining vegetable oil in a second frying pan over a medium to high heat and, when hot, crack in the eggs and fry them to your liking.

When you are sure the fried rice is hot all the way through, remove from the heat and stir through the soy sauce and sesame oil.

Serve portions of the fried rice topped with a fried egg and a sprinkling of the chilli.

TIP

Leftover rice can be rinsed in cold water and then kept in the fridge for a day, or frozen for later use.

BOLOGNAISE PASTIES

SERVES 4

What could be better than just a simple bolognaise? A bolognaise pasty, that's what! Such a simple recipe to throw together and it works well at room temperature for lunch the next day. If you don't have the time or inclination to make the pastry then just use ready-made.

PREP TIME 30 MINUTES
COOKING TIME 10 MINUTES

500g plain flour, plus
   a little extra for rolling
125g butter, cold and cubed
125g lard, cold and cubed
2 eggs
350g Bonus Bolognaise
   (page 113)
150g potatoes, scrubbed clean
   and cut into ½cm pieces
150g swede, peeled and
   cut into ½cm pieces

Tip the flour into a bowl and rub in the butter and lard until the mixture resembles breadcrumbs. Add 1 egg and about 75ml of water and work the ingredients until they come together. Tip the pastry out on to a surface, shape into a ball, wrap tightly in clingfilm and rest in the fridge for about 45 minutes.

Preheat the oven to 190°C/Gas 5 and line a baking sheet with parchment.

Mix together the bolognaise, potatoes and swede, along with a generous pinch of both salt and pepper.

Unwrap the pastry and divide into 4. Take each piece, one at a time, and roll out into a rough circular shape. Using a plate as a rough guide, cut out a circle about 22cm wide. Pile a quarter of the bolognaise mixture into the middle of the circle.

Beat the second egg and brush around the edge of the pastry. Draw the two sides of the pasty together over the filling and gently push together. Crimp the join and then place the pasty carefully on the prepared baking sheet. Repeat the process with the remaining bolognaise and pastry.

When they are all ready, brush the pasties with the remaining beaten egg and then slide the tray into the preheated oven and bake for 35 minutes, or until the pasties are dark golden brown all over.

TIP

If you don't have any bolognaise kicking about then don't worry – pasties are a great way of using up leftovers from Shakshouka (page 31) to cauliflower cheese. If you want a real crowd pleaser then load the pastry with ham, cheese and a few cheeky dollops of Branston Pickle for a perfect lunch pasty.

FRIDAY NIGHT FEASTS

VEGGIE BURGERS WITH SWEET POTATO WEDGES

SERVES 4

Don't be put off by the name – these are so tasty that it will be a good half hour after you've finished eating that you'll realise there was no meat in the burger. Kidney beans are a great source of protein and will make you feel full. This is the sort of meal that you can hide a load of veg in from the kids.

PREP TIME 20 MINUTES
COOKING TIME 50 MINUTES

———

2 x 400g tins kidney beans, drained
3 tbsp vegetable oil
1 onion, peeled and diced
75g carrot, peeled and grated
75g courgette, washed and grated
2 tsp ground cumin
3 sweet potatoes (roughly 400g), scrubbed clean, each one cut in half and then into 8 wedges
2 tbsp plain flour
4 x burger baps
50ml tomato ketchup
1 round lettuce, separated into leaves

Preheat the oven to 190°C/Gas 5.

Tip the beans into a saucepan filled with water, bring to the boil and simmer for about 10 minutes, or until the beans are very, very soft.

Whilst the beans are cooking, heat up a third of the oil in a large frying pan over a medium heat and, when hot, add the onion, carrot and courgette. Fry the ingredients, stirring regularly, for 5 minutes and then sprinkle in the cumin. Cook for a further 1 minute and then tip the mixture into a bowl to cool.

Drain the beans and add to the carrot, courgette and onion mixture. Roughly mash up the beans and mix everything together. Leave to cool a little.

Whilst the burger mix is cooling, place the wedges in a single layer on a roasting tray, season with a third of the oil and then roast in the preheated oven for 25–30 minutes, or until cooked through and lightly browned.

Whilst the sweet potatoes are cooking, shape the vegetable mixture into 4 large patties. Dust each one in a little of the flour and put to one side.

Heat the remaining oil in a large frying pan over a medium heat and cook the burgers for about 2–3 minutes on each side.

Cut the burger baps in half and place in the preheated oven very quickly to warm and then spread with the ketchup, top with the veggie burgers and lettuce, and serve with the sweet potato wedges.

Mexican Feast
FISH TACOS WITH SWEETCORN RELISH

 SERVES 4

This is a proper fancy-looking dish for less than a fiver. For some reason everyone thinks fish is expensive, but if you take a look through the frozen section at the supermarket, you'll be surprised by what you can afford. Do not be put off by frozen fish; much of it is frozen at sea just after being caught, which helps retain nutrients and flavour.

PREP TIME 15 MINUTES
COOKING TIME 25 MINUTES

———

1 red onion, peeled and
    finely sliced
1 lime, juice only
1 tbsp butter
1 white onion, peeled and diced
½ small bunch of fresh coriander,
    leaves and stalks separated
1 x 400g tin kidney beans, drained
300ml chicken stock
800g skinless pollock fillets
    (frozen and defrosted are
    perfect), cut into 8 equal pieces
1 tbsp vegetable oil
1 tsp smoked paprika
1 tsp ground cumin
1 x 200g tin sweetcorn, drained
1 red chilli, de-seeded
    and finely sliced
8 soft tacos
½ iceberg lettuce, shredded

Preheat the oven to 220°C/Gas 7.

Place the red onion in a bowl with the lime juice. Give it a little stir and then leave to sit whilst you get on with the rest of the recipe.

Heat the butter in a saucepan over a medium to high heat and, when melted and bubbling, add the white onion and fry for 5 minutes. Whilst the onion is sweating away, roughly chop the coriander stalks into small pieces and add to the pan. Fry the ingredients together for 1 minute and then add the beans and stock. Bring the whole lot to a simmer and cook for 15 minutes, stirring every now and then. The beans should slowly break down and the sauce should thicken.

Lay the pieces of fish on a baking tray.

Mix the oil with the paprika and cumin and a good pinch of both salt and pepper. Drizzle the spiced oil as equally as possible over the fish (using a pastry brush will help with this). Slide the spiced fish into the preheated oven and bake for about 12 minutes, or until you are happy the fish is fully cooked through – you can check this by gently pushing the surface of one of the fillets: if the fish is cooked then the flesh will flake easily.

Whilst the fish is cooking, mix the sweetcorn and chilli. Finely chop the coriander leaves and add to the sweetcorn mix.

Serve the fish with the beans, sweetcorn salsa, tacos and lettuce – let everybody get stuck in.

British Feast
ROAST CHICKEN WITH ALL THE TRIMMINGS

SERVES 4

There is always some meat left on the carcass of a chicken – even when you think you're just saving the carcass for stock, you're not. If you're fastidious you will find meat. Using pecorino may be more expensive than Cheddar, but there is so much more flavour that you need much less.

PREP TIME 45 MINUTES
COOKING TIME 90 MINUTES

4g dried porcini mushrooms
25g butter
1 large onion, peeled and diced
200g breadcrumbs
1 tsp dried sage
2 sprigs of fresh thyme,
  leaves only
1 egg
1 whole chicken
4 baking potatoes, scrubbed clean
1 tbsp sunflower oil
2 large carrots, peeled and
  cut into batons
250g spring greens
1 bay leaf
1 chicken stock cube
25g plain flour

Preheat the oven to 180°C/Gas 4.

Pour boiling water over the mushrooms and leave to rehydrate for 10 minutes. Once hydrated, drain them but be sure to keep the liquid. Roughly chop the mushrooms.

Heat half the butter in a large saucepan over a medium heat and, when melted and bubbling, add the onion and mushrooms and cook, stirring regularly, for 5 minutes, or until softened and lightly coloured. Sprinkle in the breadcrumbs and herbs and continue to stir and fry for a further 2 minutes. Turn off the heat but continue to stir the breadcrumbs until the mixture loosely comes together. Crack in the egg, season with a good pinch of salt and pepper and add 75ml of the mushroom soaking water. Give the whole lot a thorough mix, tip into a bowl and leave to cool a little.

Remove the string from the chicken and open up the cavity between the legs. Sprinkle in some salt and pepper and then pack in your stuffing, making sure to leave a gap between the top of the stuffing and the roof of the chicken insides. If you can't fit all the stuffing in the chicken then just roll up into balls and roast separately for 15 minutes.

Place the chicken in a roasting tray and cook in the preheated oven for roughly 1 hour and 30 minutes (depending on the size of your chicken), or until the juices run clear.

Meanwhile, rub each potato with just a little sunflower oil. When the chicken has been cooking for 30 minutes, place the potatoes on a tray and cook in the oven alongside the chicken.

Whilst the chicken and potatoes are cooking, bring a large pot of water to the boil. Drop in the carrots and boil for 5 minutes.

Prepare the spring greens by pulling them apart into individual leaves, washing them well and cutting out any thick stems.

When the carrots have had their 5 minutes simmering, add the spring greens to the pot, bring back up to the boil and simmer both together for a further 3 minutes.

Use a slotted spoon to remove the cooked vegetables to a colander to drain. Pour out all but 600ml of the vegetable cooking liquid and add the bay leaf and stock cube. Keep this liquid off the heat to one side.

When the chicken is ready, remove from the oven and carefully transfer to a plate. Cover with a layer of tin foil and then a tea towel to keep it warm.

Place the chicken roasting tray over a medium heat on the hob and stir in the flour. Cook for about 1 minute and then add a ladleful of vegetable cooking liquid. Allow the liquid to be incorporated completely before adding the next ladleful, until you have used up all the liquid. Bring the gravy to a boil and simmer for a couple of minutes to thicken.

You are now ready to serve. (If your carrots and greens have gone cold in the colander, pour a kettle of boiling water over the top of them to reheat.) Remove the potatoes from the oven, carve up the chicken and sit down to a proper £5 feast.

TIP

Never throw away bread: blitz into crumbs and keep in the freezer.

Japanese Feast
MISO SOUP

SERVES 4

Miso soup is not at all tricky to make. It's actually embarrassingly easy. The health benefits may only be circumstantial, but it is purported to be very good for you. Miso lasts a long time in the fridge so pick up a pot and have soup at your fingertips any time.

PREP TIME 2 MINUTES
COOKING TIME 5 MINUTES

50g brown miso paste
15g spring onions, finely
    sliced, to serve

Bring 800ml of water to the boil in a large saucepan.

Spoon the miso into a bowl and pour over about 200ml of the hot water, mixing the miso in to make a loose paste.

Pour the miso into the saucepan and stir.

Serve topped with the spring onions.

Japanese Feast

VEGETABLE TEMPURA FRITTERS SERVES 4

You can tempura almost anything (edible) using this recipe. Don't bother with expensive ready-made mixes – follow this instead. The trick with this recipe is in the preparation – try to cut the vegetables into similar sizes to ensure even cooking.

PREP TIME 20 MINUTES
COOKING TIME 10 MINUTES

—

150g self-raising flour
1 egg, separated
150g courgette, washed and
   cut into long, thin strips
150g carrots, peeled and cut
   into long, thin strips
1 onion, peeled and thinly sliced
about 100ml vegetable oil
2 tbsp light soy sauce
1 tbsp rice wine vinegar

Tip the flour into a bowl, add the egg yolk and whisk in enough water to make a thick, smooth batter. Whisk up the egg whites in a separate bowl until airy and frothy. Fold the whites through the batter.

Tip all the vegetables into the batter and add a good pinch of salt. Stir to coat the vegetables in the batter.

Heat up a little of the oil in a large, non-stick frying pan over a medium to high heat and, when hot, carefully add large spoonfuls of the mixture, ensuring you have a good amount of batter clinging to the vegetables. Don't overcrowd the pan – a few at a time is perfect. Fry the fritters for about 3 minutes on each side, by which time they will have browned and blown up a little.

Remove the fritters to a piece of kitchen roll to blot off any excess oil and then repeat the process with a little more oil and some of the vegetables until you have finished the mixture.

Just before serving, combine the soy sauce and vinegar and place in a bowl alongside your fritters.

Japanese Feast
MUSHROOM KATSU 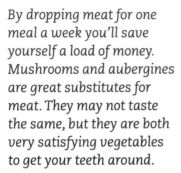 SERVES 4

By dropping meat for one meal a week you'll save yourself a load of money. Mushrooms and aubergines are great substitutes for meat. They may not taste the same, but they are both very satisfying vegetables to get your teeth around.

PREP TIME 20 MINUTES
COOKING TIME 20 MINUTES

80ml vegetable oil
1 onion, peeled and diced
75g carrot, peeled and diced
1 celery stalk, peeled and diced
1 apple, peeled and grated
1 tbsp mild curry powder
250ml vegetable stock
1 tbsp honey
2 eggs
60g plain flour
1 tsp cayenne
80g breadcrumbs
3 large Portobello mushrooms,
   brushed cleaned and
   cut in 4 lengthways
400g cooked rice, to serve
   (200g raw weight)

Heat 10ml of the oil in a saucepan over a medium to high heat. When hot, add the onion, carrot, celery and apple. Fry the vegetables for 5 minutes, or until they are nicely softened.

Sprinkle in the curry powder and fry for 1 minute, stirring almost constantly.

Pour in the stock and bring to a simmer. Cook the vegetables for 15 minutes, or until completely soft.

Add the honey and blend until smooth, adding a little water if needed. Turn off the heat and leave to one side.

Crack the eggs into a bowl and whisk them together. Sprinkle the flour on to a plate and mix in the cayenne pepper. Tip the breadcrumbs on to a third plate.

Taking one piece of mushroom at a time, dust in the spiced flour, then dip in the egg, and finally roll in the breadcrumbs to coat. Repeat the process with the remaining pieces of mushroom.

When you have coated all of the mushrooms, heat the remaining oil in a large frying pan, add the breadcrumbed mushrooms and cook until crisp and golden. Drain them on a piece of kitchen roll to dab off any remaining oil.

Serve the fried mushrooms with the katsu sauce and rice.

French Feast
MOULES MARINIÈRES WITH CHIPS

SERVES 4

This is one of those dishes that you have on holiday, when budgets don't matter and you can eat whatever you want. The good news is that mussels are incredibly good value and in the UK we produce some of the best mussels in the world. So don't wait for the holidays to come round again, get stuck into mussels any time with this recipe.

PREP TIME 10 MINUTES
COOKING TIME 30 MINUTES

1.5 litres vegetable oil
1kg potatoes, peeled and
    cut into 1cm thick chips
2 tbsp olive oil
1 onion, peeled and diced
1 clove garlic, peeled and
    finely chopped
1.5kg mussels, cleaned
100ml white wine
75ml double cream
½ small bunch of fresh
    parsley, roughly chopped

Pour the vegetable oil into a deep saucepan and place it over a medium to high heat. You want to heat the oil to 160°C. If you don't have a thermometer, then drop in a piece of bread – when the oil is hot enough, it should bubble up and take about 10 seconds to turn brown. When you are happy the oil is at the correct temperature, carefully lower some of the chipped potatoes into the oil and cook for about 10 minutes, or until you can easily push a fork into the potato. Do not overcrowd the pan – if the potatoes don't fit in comfortably then cook them in batches. Carefully scoop the blanched potatoes out of the oil and leave them to cool on a tray.

Just before you are about to eat, reheat the vegetable oil to 180°C and, in batches if needed, fry the blanched chips for 2 minutes, or until they are golden and crisp.

For the mussels, heat the olive oil in a large saucepan over a medium to high heat. When hot, add the onion and garlic, and cook, stirring regularly, for 5 minutes, or until they are nicely softened.

Tumble in the mussels, stirring them into the cooking onions. Crank up the heat to maximum, pour in the wine and clamp a lid tightly on to the pan. Cook without removing the lid for 6 minutes – during this time it is a good idea to shake the pan a little to ensure even cooking.

After 6 minutes, take the lid off the pan and the majority of mussels should be opened – discard any that stay tightly clamped shut. Add the cream and the parsley to the mussels, bring the liquid up to the boil one last time and then serve with the chips.

Thai Feast
PAD THAI   SERVES 6

This is a classic stir-fry from Thailand and is a great recipe for using up all sorts of meat and veg. Once you know the method you'll always have a go-to meal. It's a good idea to invest in certain ingredients that have a long shelf life, like fish sauce and soy sauce, as they pretty much never go off and will bring almost any dish to life. Don't chuck away limes after you've squeezed them – you can use them to flavour water or soups.

PREP TIME 10 MINUTES
COOKING TIME 10 MINUTES

—

350g dried rice noodles
1 tbsp vegetable oil
2 cloves garlic, peeled and
   finely chopped
80g spring onions, white and
   green parts, both chopped
1 red chilli, de-seeded and
   finely sliced
1 tbsp fish sauce
1 lime, juice only
½ small bunch of fresh
   coriander, roughly chopped

Cook the noodles according to the packet instructions and then drain through a colander. Run under cold water and keep to one side.

Heat the oil in a large wok or frying pan over a high heat and, when hot, quickly add the garlic, spring onions and chilli and stir-fry for 1 minute.

Add the cooked and cooled noodles to the pan and continue to stir-fry over the highest heat for 3–4 minutes, or until the noodles are hot through.

Take the pan off the heat and toss through the fish sauce, lime juice and coriander leaves.

TIP

Hang on to citrus peeling for homemade flavoured water.

Thai Feast
THAI BASIL AUBERGINE

SERVES **6**

Don't obsess about cooking in olive oil or sunflower oil just because they sound nicer. They are all pretty much the same at high temperatures, so just opt for the cheapest.

PREP TIME 15 MINUTES
COOKING TIME 15 MINUTES

1 tbsp vegetable oil
1 star anise
½ tsp dried chilli flakes
3 cloves garlic, peeled
   and finely chopped
175g minced pork
400g aubergine, cut
   into 3cm chunks
150g courgette, cut
   into 3cm chunks
2 tbsp light soy sauce
1 tsp fish sauce
½ small bunch of fresh
   basil, leaves only, chopped
1 spring onion, finely sliced
75g peanuts, roughly chopped

Heat the oil in a large saucepan over a medium to high heat. When hot, add the star anise, chilli and garlic and stir-fry for 2 minutes.

Crumble in the minced pork, breaking it up in the pan with a wooden spoon as it fries.

Add the aubergine and courgette along with 100ml of water, cover and cook for 10 minutes, or until the aubergine and courgette are both very tender.

Turn the heat off under the pan and season with the soy and fish sauces.

Serve topped with the basil leaves, spring onion and peanuts.

TIP

Try to keep herbs in their original packaging for as long as possible, only opening them as you need them. This will preserve the gases the herbs are packed in and increase shelf life. Spices can go off so are best kept in airtight containers.

Pizza Feast
FAMILY PIZZA

SERVES 6

Basic pizza dough doesn't have to prove for hours and is great for getting kids of all ages involved in cooking. There is no right or wrong to the shape – just try to roll it out to an even thickness.

PREP TIME 20 MINUTES,
PLUS 60 MINUTES RISING
COOKING TIME 20 MINUTES

———

6 tsp baking powder
1kg plain flour, plus a little
    extra for dusting
225g tinned chopped tomatoes
1 clove garlic, peeled
1 tsp dried oregano
½ small bunch of fresh basil
50g tomato puree
150g Cheddar, grated
1 red onion, peeled and
    finely sliced
1 red pepper, de-seeded
    and finely sliced
100g mushrooms, brushed
    clean and finely sliced
200g cooked chicken breast
1 tbsp olive oil

Sieve the baking powder and flour into a bowl and gradually stir in 500ml water until you reach a sticky dough. Tip out on to a lightly floured surface and knead for 2 minutes. Place the dough into a clean bowl, cover with clingfilm and leave to sit for 60 minutes.

Place the tomatoes, garlic, oregano, basil stalks and tomato puree in a small food processor and blitz until you reach a smooth sauce.

Preheat the oven to 200°C/Gas 6.

Tip the dough out on to your surface and divide into two large balls. Nip a little piece of dough from each large ball, about the size of a golfball, and reserve for the dessert calzone. Take one of the large balls and, using a rolling pin, roll out into a rough rectangle – about 30 x 15cm, or the size of your biggest baking tray. The shape isn't too important, but try to roll the dough out to an even thickness.

Carefully lay the dough on your baking tray, pushing it out and reshaping with your fingers as need be. Spread half of the tomato sauce over the pizza and then dress with half of the cheese, onion, pepper, mushrooms and chicken, or toppings of your choice. Slide the tray into the preheated oven and bake for 15 minutes, or until coloured, crisp and golden on top.

Whilst the first pizza is baking, prepare your second pizza, using the other large ball of pizza dough and the remaining toppings. As soon as the first pizza comes out, slide the second savoury pizza in. Dress each cooked pizza with half the basil leaves and oil before serving.

Pizza Feast
BANANA & CHOCOLATE CALZONE

SERVES **6**

PREP TIME 10 MINUTES
COOKING TIME 25 MINUTES

—

reserved pizza dough
(page 167)
180g chocolate spread
2 bananas, peeled and
cut into 2cm chunks

To make the dessert calzone, take the small reserved dough balls and roll each one into a neat circle.

Spread with the chocolate and divide the banana pieces between the two. Close each calzone by folding one edge over the filling and pressing into the far edge to seal.

Bake the calzones in the preheated oven for 25 minutes.

Chinese Feast
CHICKEN & SWEETCORN SOUP

SERVES 4

This is a takeaway classic that usually looks as though it comes from a different world where soup is the consistency of thick cream. Fear not, this is an incredibly easy recipe that packs all the flavour without the gloopy texture.

PREP TIME 45 MINUTES
COOKING TIME 90 MINUTES

300g chicken bones (from a roast chicken carcass)
2cm ginger, peeled and roughly chopped
outer leaves of 2 onions (60g)
125g creamed sweetcorn
1 egg
1 tbsp soy sauce
1 tsp sesame oil
1 tsp cornflour

Place the chicken bones in a large saucepan and cover with about 1.5 litres of water. Add the ginger and onion leaves, bring to the boil and leave to simmer for about 1 hour.

Strain this chicken stock into a jug, discarding the bones but keeping back the boiled ginger. Measure 700ml of stock into a saucepan over a medium to high heat, then pour in the sweetcorn.

Crack the egg into a bowl and whisk with the soy sauce, sesame oil and cornflour.

When the soup has come to the boil, reduce the heat to medium and then whisk the egg mixture in. The soup will thicken up and the egg will disperse and cook almost instantly. When you are happy the ingredients are all well combined, slowly bring the soup back up to the boil and then serve.

TIP

Peel ginger with a teaspoon – it will follow the contours of the ginger, which reduces wastage.

Chinese Feast
EGG-FRIED RICE

SERVES 4

If cooking this as part of a Chinese feast, use the ginger from the Chicken and Sweetcorn Soup (page 172).

PREP TIME 10 MINUTES
COOKING TIME 25 MINUTES
———

125g long grain rice
1 egg
1 tbsp sunflower oil
2 spring onions, sliced
2cm ginger, peeled and
   finely chopped
1 clove garlic, peeled and
   finely chopped
100g carrots, peeled and diced
60g frozen peas
1 tbsp soy sauce
1 tsp sesame oil

Cook the rice according to the packet instructions and then tip on to a baking tray and leave to cool uncovered.

Crack the egg into a bowl and give it a whisk.

Heat a little bit of the sunflower oil in a large frying pan over a high heat and, when hot, pour in the egg and let it fry hard for 1 minute on each side until fully cooked and lightly golden. Remove the egg to a board.

Add the remaining sunflower oil to the pan and, when it is hot, add the onions, ginger and garlic to the pan, along with the carrot. Stir-fry for 2 minutes then chuck in the frozen peas and toss the whole lot together.

Scrape the cooled rice into the pan and fry with the vegetables for 2 minutes, until the rice is piping hot.

Take the pan from the heat, roughly chop the fried egg into pieces and stir through the rice, along with the soy sauce and sesame oil.

TIP

Never throw away the green part of a spring onion; it is full of flavour.

Chinese Feast
SWEET & SOUR PORK

SERVES 4

Even a quick 5-minute marinade will help the meat take on a lot more flavour. This is especially useful when dealing with lean meat that can often be light on taste.

PREP TIME 10 MINUTES
COOKING TIME 15 MINUTES

450g pork tenderloin,
    cut into 3cm chunks
65ml light soy sauce
1 tbsp sunflower oil
1 red onion, peeled and
    roughly chopped
1 red pepper, de-seeded
    and finely sliced
1 green pepper, de-seeded
    and finely sliced
1 clove garlic, peeled and
    finely chopped
25g caster sugar
2 tbsp red wine vinegar
2 tbsp tomato ketchup
½ tbsp sesame oil
3 spring onions, sliced
    to garnish

Lay the pork pieces in a dish and pour over 50ml of the soy sauce. Give the ingredients a good mix, to try and cover the meat as thoroughly as possible, and then leave for a quick marinade.

Meanwhile, place the sunflower oil in a large, non-stick frying pan over a medium to high heat and, when hot, add the red onion and both the peppers. Stir-fry for 2 minutes and then add the garlic. Continue to stir-fry for a further minute and then add the marinated pork. Continue to stir-fry for about 4 minutes, or until you are happy it is cooked through.

Sprinkle in the sugar and stir until it begins to melt.

Pour in the vinegar and let it steam up and evaporate to almost nothing.

Turn the heat right down, shake in the tomato ketchup and add the remaining soy sauce, along with the sesame oil.

Give the whole lot one last stir and then garnish with the spring onions before serving with egg-fried rice (page 173).

Indian Feast LAMB CURRY

SERVES 4

For some reason most people think that you need a stockpile of spices, tandoors and ancient recipes to produce a decent curry at home. It simply isn't true – just a few basic spices will do. With a cheap cut of meat and this recipe, you can stop relying on the takeaway.

PREP TIME 15 MINUTES
COOKING TIME 90 MINUTES

2 tbsp olive oil
2 onions, peeled and diced
4 cloves garlic, peeled
 and chopped
1 cinnamon stick
1 tbsp garam masala
2 tsp ground turmeric
1 tbsp curry powder
1kg lamb neck, cut into
 3cm chunks
1 x 400g tin chopped tomatoes
200ml chicken stock
½ small bunch of fresh
 coriander, leaves only,
 chopped – use the stalks
 in the Daal (facing page)

Heat the oil in a pan and fry the onions, garlic and cinnamon stick together for 5 minutes.

Sprinkle in the garam masala, turmeric and curry powder and fry for a further minute, stirring regularly.

Add the lamb to the pan and stir into the rest of the ingredients.

Pour in the tomatoes and stock and bring to a simmer. Leave to cook for about 1½ hours, or until the meat is meltingly tender.

Sprinkle the coriander leaves over the curry just before serving.

TIP

Consider using fruits to flavour a curry – apples and bananas work well.

Indian Feast
DAAL  SERVES 4

*Lentils are the mainstay
ingredient for millions of
people throughout Asia
and I can see why – they are
not just filling but also are a
wonderful vehicle for flavour,
soaking up spice and stock,
resulting in a wonderfully
satisfying dish. The difference
between an average daal and
a great one is the addition
of freshly cooked ingredients
right at the very end.*

PREP TIME 10 MINUTES,
PLUS OVERNIGHT SOAKING
COOKING TIME 45 MINUTES

1–2 tbsp olive oil
2 cinnamon sticks
3 bay leaves
1 tsp cumin seeds
1 onion, peeled and diced
4 cloves garlic, peeled
  and diced
1½ tbsp garam masala
½ tbsp ground turmeric
1 tsp chilli powder
150g chana daal, soaked
  overnight
500–750ml chicken or
  vegetable stock
1 green chilli
2 tsp mustard seeds
½ small bunch of coriander,
  stalks only, chopped –
  use the leaves in the Lamb
  Curry (facing page)

Heat a little of the oil in a large saucepan and add
the cinnamon sticks, bay leaves, cumin seeds, half
the onion and all of the garlic. Fry for about 5 minutes,
stirring regularly. Sprinkle in one tablespoon of the
garam masala, all the turmeric and chilli powder
and fry for another minute.

Drain the chana daal and add to the pan. Pour in
500ml of stock and bring up to a simmer.

Split the green chilli down the middle and then add to
the pan. Simmer the chana daal for about 40 minutes,
or until tender, adding more stock, if needed.

When the lentils are cooked, turn the heat off and
then heat the remaining oil in a separate frying pan
over a medium to high heat. Add the remaining
onion and cook for 2 minutes.

Chuck in the mustard seeds, the remaining garam
masala and the coriander and fry for about 3 minutes.

Pour the fried ingredients into the cooked daal then
serve up.

 TIP

*Don't automatically assume dried pulses
will be cheaper than tinned ones – often the
dried ones are more expensive.*

Indian Feast
CHAPPATTIS

 SERVES 4

Chappattis are incredibly simple to make – just three ingredients, a bit of wrist work and you have yourself fresh bread. Simples.

PREP TIME 10 MINUTES
COOKING TIME 10 MINUTES

250g wholemeal flour,
   plus a little extra for dusting
a good sprinkling of salt

Tip the flour into a bowl and add the salt.

Gradually pour in about 150ml warm water from the tap (you may need a little more or a little less), mixing as you go, until you reach a slightly sticky dough.

Dust a clean surface with a little extra flour and knead the dough for about 5 minutes. Roll the dough into a ball and rest in a clean bowl for 10 minutes.

Divide the dough into 8 (roughly) equal-sized balls and flatten slightly with the palm of your hand. Roll each one into a disc about ½cm thick.

Fry the chappattis in a dry pan for 30–45 seconds on each side.

Serve with Lamb Curry, Daal and Roasted Cauliflower (pages 176–7 and opposite).

Indian Feast
ROASTED CAULIFLOWER

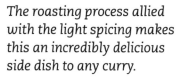

The roasting process allied with the light spicing makes this an incredibly delicious side dish to any curry.

PREP TIME 10 MINUTES
COOKING TIME 35 MINUTES

—

2 tbsp olive oil
1 cauliflower, florets only
1 tbsp curry powder
1 tsp salt

Preheat the oven to 200°C/Gas 6.

Pour the oil into a roasting tray and slide the tray into the preheated oven to heat up for 10 minutes. Remove the tray from the oven and carefully drop in the cauliflower florets.

Roast for 15 minutes.

Take the tray out of the oven and sprinkle over the curry powder and salt. Turn the cauliflower in the oil and spices and then return the tray to the oven and roast for a further 10 minutes.

Serve with Lamb Curry, Daal and Chappattis (page 176–7 and opposite).

Spanish Feast
SPICED MEATBALLS

SERVES
4-6

Why blow the budget using more expensive beef mince when making meatballs – once they've been spiced and had breadcrumbs and egg added to them you'd be hard pushed to tell the difference in flavour, and your teenage kids certainly won't. A few raisins in the meat will sweeten things up a little to encourage younger children and adults alike to try new flavours.

PREP TIME 15 MINUTES
COOKING TIME 40 MINUTES

600g minced pork
80g breadcrumbs
1 egg
½ tsp ground cinnamon
25g raisins
½ small bunch of fresh basil,
    leaves and stalks separated
1 tbsp vegetable oil
2 cloves garlic, peeled and
    roughly chopped
1 red onion, peeled and diced
1 red pepper, de-seeded
    and cut into long strips
1 tbsp red wine vinegar
1 x 400g tin chopped tomatoes
35g almonds, roughly chopped
    (optional)

Tip the minced pork into a bowl and add the breadcrumbs, egg, cinnamon and raisins, along with a generous pinch of both salt and pepper. Finely chop up the basil stalks and chuck them in, too. Get your hands stuck in and pummel the ingredients together, making sure they are well combined.

Using wet hands, shape the mixture into about 12 balls (roughly 50g each). Place on a tray and leave in the fridge for 10 minutes to firm up.

Heat the oil in a large, wide pan over a medium to high heat and, when hot, add the garlic, onion and pepper and sweat, stirring regularly, for about 10 minutes, or until the ingredients begin to soften.

Crank up the heat to maximum and pour in the vinegar – this will bubble up and reduce to almost nothing. Add the tin of tomatoes and then half fill the tin with water and add this, too. Mix all the ingredients together and leave to simmer for 3 minutes, seasoning with salt and pepper.

Gently drop the meatballs into the sauce, don't worry if it feels a little crowded. Once they are in the sauce, bring the liquid back to a simmer and cook for 12–15 minutes, or until you are sure the meat is cooked through. You can check this by cutting open one of the balls and making sure the raw pink flesh has turned white.

Serve the meatballs topped with the almonds and basil leaves.

Spanish Feast
PATATAS BRAVAS

SERVES 4-6

Spuds remain one of the best ways to fill up hungry tummies, and don't forget they have a nutritional value, too, especially if you don't peel them. They may not count towards your 5 a day, but they do contain a good amount of dietary fibre, potassium and vitamin B. If you have tomatoes that you think are on the turn, then use them here – they'll be sweeter and easier to cook.

PREP TIME 15 MINUTES
COOKING TIME 40 MINUTES

———

500g potatoes, scrubbed
   clean and roughly cut
   into 4cm chunks
2 tbsp vegetable oil
1 small onion, peeled and sliced
3 anchovy fillets (about 10g),
   drained and roughly chopped
1 tbsp tomato puree
½ tsp smoked paprika
1 x 400g tin chopped tomatoes
½ small bunch of fresh parsley,
   roughly chopped

Bring a large pot of water to the boil and, when bubbling, cook the potatoes for about 20 minutes, or until they are soft enough for a fork to push in easily. Quickly drain in a colander and then tip on to a tray to steam dry for about 15 minutes.

Whilst the potatoes are drying, heat the oil in a large frying pan over a medium to high heat. When hot, add the onion slices and fry gently, stirring regularly, for about 8 minutes, or until they begin to soften – try not to colour them too much. Add the anchovy and stir in.

Turn up the heat to maximum and, when sizzling, slide in the dried potatoes and fry with the onions – don't move them too much to avoid them breaking up.

When the potatoes have browned a little, gently stir in the tomato puree and smoked paprika. Again, being careful not to break up the spuds

Pour in the chopped tomatoes, bring them up to a simmer, season with salt and pepper and then take off the heat.

Serve the potatoes with a good sprinkling of parsley.

Spanish Feast
POLENTA MASH

SERVES 4-6

Bored of mash? Well, even if you're not, this is a great alternative. Any leftover polenta can be laid in a tray lined with clingfilm, cooled and cut into squares the next day to be roasted for a great base to a salad. The best news? Polenta is cheap, cheap, cheap.

PREP TIME 5 MINUTES
COOKING TIME 20 MINUTES

250ml milk
5 sage leaves, finely sliced
250g quick cook polenta
grating of nutmeg
50g Parmesan, grated

Pour the milk into a large pan and place over a medium heat. Add the sage and a good pinch of both salt and pepper.

When the milk comes to the boil, turn down the heat, pour in the polenta and begin whisking and stirring for your life. The mixture will thicken up quickly, so it's best to start with a whisk and then move on to a wooden spoon. Cook the polenta over a low heat, stirring almost constantly, for about 8 minutes, by which time it will have thickened up and lost its grainy consistency.

Take off the heat and stir in the nutmeg and Parmesan.

Serve with a good grinding of black pepper.

Kids' Feast
MINI BURGERS

The best type of kids' party food is the kind that both kids and adults enjoy. That way, the grown ups can hoover up the leftovers! The breadcrumbs in the recipe not only bulk out the meat, but also help absorb the cooking juices, which gives a more succulent burger.

PREP TIME 15 MINUTES
COOKING TIME 30 MINUTES
—

1.5kg minced beef
200g breadcrumbs
1 onion, very finely chopped
1 egg
2 small round lettuces,
    leaves separated
4 tomatoes, sliced thinly
30 x mini burger buns
ketchup, to serve
mustard, to serve

Put the beef, breadcrumbs, onion and egg into a bowl and mix together thoroughly until combined.

Using wet hands so that the mix doesn't stick, shape into 30 small burgers (roughly 50g each).

Heat a large griddle pan over a medium to high heat and, when hot, cook the burgers in batches for about 4 minutes on each side.

Serve the burgers in a mini bun with a leaf of lettuce, a slice of tomato and a splodge of ketchup or mustard.

Kids' Feast
SAUSAGE ROLLS

MAKES
30

Stop buying cheap, high-street sausage rolls and make your own at home. They're so easy and are cheaper, too. Make sure to use cold puff pastry, as it will be easier to work with and will puff up better. Add nuts and dried fruit for a fancier sausage roll, or even brush the puff with English mustard for a more adult version.

PREP TIME 25 MINUTES
COOKING TIME 40 MINUTES

600g sausage meat
1 small bunch of fresh parsley,
   finely chopped
1 x 375g packet puff pastry
2 eggs
1 tsp onion seeds (nigella seeds)

Preheat the oven to 200°C/Gas 6.

Mix the sausage meat and parsley in a bowl until well combined.

Roll the pastry out on a lightly floured surface to a size about 35 x 20cm. Cut the sheet lengthways into three equal strips.

Divide the sausage mixture into 3 and roughly shape each third into a long sausage. Lay each one just to the side of centre on each length of pastry. Adjust the meat so that is goes all the way to the ends of the pastry and is roughly the same diameter all the way down.

Beat the eggs in a bowl and brush down the length of each pastry strip, just to the side of the sausage meat. Roll one side of the pastry over the meat to join the other side and push down gently with your fingers to seal.

Brush the egg wash all over the pastry and place the 3 giant sausage rolls in the fridge for 10 minutes.

After 10 minutes brush the sausage rolls again and sprinkle with the onion seeds. Cut each of the large rolls into 10 and then place on to a baking sheet – don't overcrowd them, use two sheets if needed.

Bake in the oven for 25–30 minutes, or until the pastry has risen and is golden and the sausage meat is cooked through. Leave to cool slightly before serving.

Kids' Feast BRUSCHETTA

MAKES **15**

Bruschetta was originally designed for olive oil purveyors to show off their wares. The stale bread was drenched in the oil for prospective customers to try before they bought. It has now become a delicious stalwart of the Italian kitchen. It's a brilliant way of using up old bread that you think has passed its best – simply toasting to golden brown revives the texture and adds an extra tasty dimension. Because this recipe is cheap, try pushing the boat out and use more expensive bread – ciabatta or sourdough both work wonderfully well.

PREP TIME 15 MINUTES
COOKING TIME 10 MINUTES

---

8 very ripe tomatoes
2 tbsp red wine vinegar
4 shallots, peeled and
    finely sliced
3 tsp sugar
3 anchovy fillets (roughly 10g),
    drained and chopped
2 small bunches of fresh
    parsley, roughly chopped
15 slices of ciabatta
200ml olive oil
3 large cloves garlic
1 large bunch of fresh basil,
    leaves separated, to serve

Put your grill on to preheat to its highest setting.

Bring a pan of water to the boil. Make a small cross with a knife at the base of each tomato and cut out the 'eye'. When the water is boiling, drop the tomatoes into the pan and turn the heat off. Leave the tomatoes for about 45 seconds or until you see the skin start to unfurl. Immediately drain the tomatoes and cool under cold running water.

Use a small knife to peel the skin from the tomatoes and then roughly chop into large 2–3cm chunks. Place them in a bowl with the vinegar, shallots, sugar, anchovies and parsley, along with a good grinding of both salt and pepper. Leave the mix to one side.

Drizzle each slice of bread with a little olive oil then toast under the preheated grill until dark golden brown on both sides.

Peel the garlic cloves and, when the toast is ready, rub the garlic on to one side of the toast – the bread will act as a grater and the garlic will flavour the bread. Drizzle each slice of toast with a good glug of the oil.

Chop each slice in half (to make them bite-sized), dress with basil and serve.

SOMETHING SWEET

BREAD & BUTTER PUDDING

This is a dish that, although cheap, does not compromise on flavour. It's the classic way of using up slightly stale bread. In fact, it is better baked with old bread as it serves better as a mop for the custard. You can alter this basic recipe to use anything from stale croissants or muffins instead of bread, to chocolate instead of raisins.

PREP TIME 25 MINUTES
COOKING TIME 30 MINUTES

——

2 tbsp butter
8 slices of white bread,
    crusts removed (optional)
75g sultanas
3 eggs
400ml milk
100ml double cream
1 tsp vanilla extract
90g caster sugar
25g demerara sugar

Preheat the oven to 170°C/Gas 3.

Butter each slice of bread on one side and then cut into triangle-shaped quarters.

Stack up the slices in a deep baking dish, overlapping them all the way down the length of the dish – don't worry too much about how neat your bread is stacked or if there are little gaps, this is a rough and ready recipe.

Scatter the sultanas over the top, poking at least half of them under the bread slices.

Whisk together the eggs, milk, cream, vanilla extract and caster sugar in a jug and then pour over the bread.

Slide the pudding into the preheated oven and bake for 25 minutes.

Let it sit for 5 minutes and then sprinkle with the demerara sugar before serving.

TIP

Remember to hoard bread crusts in the freezer. Any time you need breadcrumbs you can blitz them from frozen and they will defrost almost instantly.

LEMON POSSET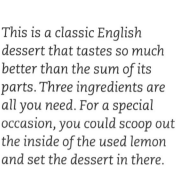

This is a classic English dessert that tastes so much better than the sum of its parts. Three ingredients are all you need. For a special occasion, you could scoop out the inside of the used lemon and set the dessert in there.

PREP TIME 5 MINUTES
COOKING TIME 5 MINUTES,
PLUS 2 HOURS COOLING

—

425ml double cream
80g caster sugar
juice and zest of 2 lemons

Gently heat the cream and sugar together, until the sugar has completely dissolved. Carefully bring to the boil and simmer for 3 minutes, then turn off the heat.

Add the lemon juice and almost all of the lemon zest to the cream (keep a little back for decoration) and give it a whisk to make sure it is thoroughly mixed.

Pour the mixture into 4 small glasses or ramekins and place in the fridge for a minimum of 2 hours, or until the cream has fully set.

Just before serving, sprinkle with the little reserved lemon zest and then get stuck in.

TIP

Microwaving lemons for 20 seconds before squeezing will help you get more juice out. Alternatively, you can roll the fruit under the palm of your hand.

BLACKCURRANT POACHED PEARS

SERVES 4

Using cordial is a cheap and effective way of getting flavour into fruits when poaching. And spices are your friend: they give huge amounts of flavour to bland foods. Vanilla extract may be more expensive than essence, but drop for drop it's much better value as it has a richer flavour.

PREP TIME 15 MINUTES
COOKING TIME 30 MINUTES

—

150ml blackcurrant cordial
1 star anise
100g caster sugar
4 pears, peeled
2 tsp vanilla extract
100g mascarpone
25g icing sugar

Pour the cordial into a pan and add the star anise, caster sugar and 400ml of water.

Bring the liquid to the boil and carefully lower in the pears. Turn down the heat and simmer the pears for about 20 minutes, or until they are tender all the way through (cooking time will depend on how ripe the pears are).

Remove the pears from the liquid and leave, covered, in a cool place.

Continue to simmer the liquid until it has reduced by two thirds – it should be glossy and thick. Remove the star anise and stir in half of the vanilla extract. Leave the liquid to cool.

Meanwhile, beat the remaining vanilla extract into the mascarpone and icing sugar until well combined.

Serve the poached pears with a quenelle of vanilla mascarpone and a good drizzle of blackcurrant sauce.

FRUITBOWL LEFTOVER LOLLIES SERVES 6

There's no excuse to throw away fruit, especially when you have a recipe this easy. There's no rule to it, pretty much any soft fruit can be blitzed up, frozen and made into delicious lollipops. Although they do contain some sugar, at least you know it is balanced out by the fruit. If you don't have a lollipop mould then simply freeze in disposable plastic containers and prod a wooden skewer in.

PREP TIME 4 MINUTES
COOKING TIME OVERNIGHT
FREEZING
——

300ml apple juice
100g caster sugar
300g soft fruit – I like raspberries, strawberries and blackberries

Place all the ingredients in a jug blender and blitz until smooth.

Pour the fruit mix into lollipop moulds and freeze overnight.

When ready to eat, dip the mould briefly in warm water to loosen the lollies and then pull them out and enjoy.

TIP

Berries going a bit squishy? Use them to make a delicious fruit smoothie.

LEMON CORDIAL SORBET

SERVES 4

As if sorbet wasn't easy enough already, this recipe has just removed any need to squeeze the fruit! We all have some sort of cordial in the cupboard, so why not try something different and turn it into a refreshing and sophisticated sorbet? If you want to be particularly fancy, you could stir through a bit of gin or prosecco and turn it into an adult pudding.

PREP TIME 10 MINUTES
COOKING TIME 5 MINUTES,
PLUS 4 HOURS FREEZING

———

350ml water
125g caster sugar
200ml lemon cordial
   (barley, if possible)

Put the water and sugar into a saucepan over a medium to high heat and bring to the boil, stirring, to dissolve the sugar in the water.

When you are happy that the sugar is fully dissolved, take the pan from the heat and stir in the lemon cordial.

Pour the liquid into a plastic container and leave to cool to room temperature.

Place the liquid in your freezer and leave to freeze for 1 hour, then give it a good whisk and put back into the freezer. Whisk the sorbet regularly, every 30 minutes or so, from that point on and for the next 2 hours, or until the liquid has completely frozen.

Serve in small glass bowls.

JELLY MOUNTAIN

SERVES
15

Simple, cheap, effective and fun – what else could you possibly want for a kids' party! Buying a savarin mould may not be cheap, but it will be yours forever and you can use it again and again. If you want a bargain then look in charity shops where you can pick one up for a fraction of its original price. Make this recipe your own – decorate with crumbled biscuits, use a different flavour of ice cream, add nuts, chopped chocolate bars, marshmallows – whatever takes your fancy.

PREP TIME 10 MINUTES,
PLUS OVERNIGHT SETTING
COOKING TIME 5 MINUTES

—

20 gelatine leaves
300ml cherry cordial
175g sugar
1x 500ml tub chocolate
   ice cream
20g hundreds and thousands

Place the gelatine leaves in a bowl, cover with cold water and leave to bloom for a minimum of 10 minutes.

Meanwhile, heat the cherry cordial with the sugar and 1.7 litres of water in a large pan over a medium to high heat. Stir until the sugar is fully dissolved, and then turn off the heat.

Pick out the gelatine leaves from the water bowl, give them a squeeze to remove the excess liquid and then stir them into the cherry liquid until dissolved.

Leave the mix to cool to room temperature and then pour into a large savarin mould. Place in the fridge and leave to set overnight.

When ready to serve, fill a large saucepan with water and heat until just below boiling point. Carefully sit the savarin mould in the hot water for about 30 seconds to loosen the sides. Place a serving plate on top and then, with a flick of the wrist, flip the mould and plate over.

Remove the jelly from the mould, pile up the middle with ice cream, sprinkle with hundreds and thousands and serve.

BANOFFEE PIE

SERVES 4

This is a great way to use up broken biscuits. Feel free to mix up the type – you don't have to stick to digestives. The blacker the banana, the sweeter it is, so don't base your opinion on its looks. If you use a particularly black banana, though, you might want to layer the whipped cream over the top, instead of underneath.

PREP TIME 10 MINUTES
COOKING TIME 2 HOURS

---

1 x 397g tin condensed milk
80g digestive biscuits
1½ tbsp butter, melted
80ml double cream
1 banana

Boil the tin of condensed milk for 2 hours and then carefully remove from the pan and leave to cool completely.

Whilst the milk is boiling, blitz the biscuits with the butter in a food processor until the mixture resembles wet sand. Divide between 4 small ramekins and leave to set in the fridge for 10 minutes.

Meanwhile, whip the cream to soft peaks, and peel and slice the banana thinly.

When ready to serve, open the tin of condensed milk, which will have turned into caramel, and spoon a quarter of the rich mix on to each of the biscuit bases. Top the caramel with a little whipped cream and finish with the sliced bananas.

TIP

Condensed milk is much cheaper than buying the ready-made caramel – all you need to do is boil it in the tin. Just be sure to follow the timings above.

CHURROS

This is a classic Spanish snack, easy to make and ready to rock your tastebuds. Don't worry if you can't find dark chocolate. It is tasty but so, too, is milk chocolate, which is also cheaper. If you're struggling to find a piping bag then you can make a quick one by cutting a hole in the corner of a sandwich bag – not perfect, but it'll work well enough for a batch of churros.

PREP TIME 10 MINUTES
COOKING TIME 15 MINUTES

150g self-raising flour
⅓ tsp baking powder
500ml vegetable oil, for frying
1 tsp ground cinnamon
100g sugar
125g dark chocolate

Put a kettle on to boil.

Tip the flour and baking powder into a bowl. Let the kettle water cool for 5 minutes and then pour it into the flour, stirring with a wooden spoon. Beat the ingredients together to form a sticky dough and then put this to one side for a few minutes.

Pour the oil into a large saucepan and begin heating to 180°C. Squeeze a tiny bit of dough into the oil and if it rises to the surface and browns straight away it is ready to go.

Mix the cinnamon and sugar together in a bowl and then tip out on to a large baking tray – the cooked churros will go into this mix to be dredged after frying.

Melt the chocolate in the microwave – zapping it with short bursts.

Attach a star-shaped nozzle to the end of a piping bag and load in the dough. Carefully squeeze out lengths of dough directly into the hot oil – you are aiming for the churros to be 8–10cm. Snip off the end of the dough with scissors, if necessary. You can probably fry about 6 churros at a time. Fry for about 3 minutes and then remove to kitchen roll to dab off the excess oil, before tipping immediately into the sugar and cinnamon mixture to coat.

Pile the churros high and serve with the melted chocolate.

NEW-YORK-STYLE YOGHURT CHEESECAKE

SERVES 4

If you want to know if an egg is OK to eat then put it in a glass of water – if it floats then throw it out, but if it sinks it's still OK.

PREP TIME 10 MINUTES
COOKING TIME 20 MINUTES

———

100g digestive biscuits
25g butter, melted
350g sweetened yoghurt
70g caster sugar
½ tsp vanilla extract
1 tbsp cornflour
2 eggs

Preheat the oven to 140°C/Gas 1 and put a kettle on to boil.

Blitz the biscuits in a food processor until they are small crumbs. Mix in the butter and then divide the mixture equally between 4 ramekins, pushing the crumbs firmly into the base.

Beat all the remaining ingredients together and divide between the lined ramekins. Place the little dishes in a large roasting dish and then pour enough boiled water from the kettle to reach about 1cm up the sides of the ramekins.

Slide the tray into the preheated oven and bake for about 20 minutes, or until the topping has just set. Remove from the oven and leave to cool.

TIP

If you think your biscuits are too soft to serve, then just run them through a hot oven for a few minutes and they will stiffen up. Leftover yoghurt can be added in place of milk to cake mixes.

BANANA FRITTERS WITH TOFFEE SAUCE

 SERVES 4

Naughty! That's the only way to describe this pud. Even if you're not into bananas, this sauce will make anything from a baked apple to roasted pineapple taste amazing.

PREP TIME 5 MINUTES
COOKING TIME 10 MINUTES

—

100ml sunflower oil,
  for frying
75g caster sugar
1 tbsp butter
50ml double cream
2 bananas, peeled
40g self-raising flour
40g cornflour

Pour the oil into a deep frying pan so that it reaches about 1cm up the side, and place the pan over a low heat.

Meanwhile, tip the sugar into a thick-based frying pan over a medium to high heat, spreading it out as evenly as possible. Leave the sugar to caramelise over the heat without stirring. When the sugar has become liquid-like and dark brown in colour, remove the pan from the heat. Carefully add the butter, swirling it in and then swirl in the cream. Keep this toffee sauce to one side.

Cut the bananas in half lengthways.

Tip the two flours into a bowl and whisk in about 100ml of water to create a thin batter.

Increase the heat under the oil and bring the temperature up to about 170°C. If you don't have a thermometer to test this, drop a little batter into the oil – it should puff up and rise to the surface immediately.

Take each banana half and dip it into the batter and then carefully lay them, one at a time, in the hot oil. Repeat the process until you have all four slices frying away in the oil. Fry them for about 90 seconds on each side, or until they are golden and crisp.

Remove the cooked fruit to a clean piece of kitchen roll to remove any excess oil and then serve topped with the toffee sauce.

TIP

Wrap the top of your bananas with cling film to make them last longer. And don't store them in the fridge – they will go black. Keep them somewhere cool, but not refrigerated.

FRUIT & TEA CAKE

SERVES 6

It may seem over the top to start saving the dregs from your tea to make a cake, but every little really does help. And actually, if you're a parent, you'll surely remember the gallons of cold tea poured down the drain – now is your chance to put that tea to good use. Even if you don't save cold tea, this recipe can be made using 2 teabags, or you can recycle 4 old bags.

PREP TIME 15 MINUTES
COOKING TIME 1 HOUR

300g raisins
250ml hot black tea
100g softened butter
175g soft, light brown sugar
1 tsp ground cinnamon
1 tsp ground mixed spice
2 eggs
350g self-raising flour
butter, to serve

Preheat the oven to 170°C/Gas 3 and line a 1-litre loaf tin.

Tip the raisins into a bowl and pour over the tea. Leave the raisins to plump up in the liquid for about 10 minutes.

Whilst the raisins are bathing, beat the softened butter and sugar together until they are fully combined and a soft, lightly pale colour.

Stir in the spices and then whisk in the eggs (don't worry too much if the mixture curdles as it will come back together).

Add the soaked fruit along with the tea and then stir in the flour.

Spoon the mixture into the prepared tin and bake in the preheated oven for 55 minutes, or until a skewer poked into the centre of the cake comes out clean.

Leave the cake to cool and then serve thick slices spread with butter.

TIP

Put a piece of bread or some apple slices in with your brown sugar – it helps to soak up the moisture and will keep the sugar soft and stop it going clumpy and unusable.

BANANA & CHOCOLATE BREAD

SERVES 6

You can't beat a good banana – they're cheap, filling and always available. The only problem is that we often buy them out of habit and not need, so many households have a glut of the wonderful yellow fruit, slowly turning brown and then black. It's very convenient then that for this recipe the darker and softer the banana, the tastier the loaf.

PREP TIME 20 MINUTES
COOKING TIME 45 MINUTES

—

125g softened butter
125g caster sugar
3 eggs
3 old, very ripe bananas,
  peeled
270g self-raising flour
100g dark chocolate,
  broken into pieces

Preheat the oven to 170°C/Gas 3 and line a 1-litre loaf tin.

Beat the butter and sugar together until the ingredients are combined and lightly pale.

Beat in the eggs one at a time – don't worry if the mix splits as it will come back together.

Roughly mash the bananas in a separate bowl, adding a splash of milk to loosen if needed and then beat the banana mix into the butter and sugar mixture, until all the ingredients are well combined.

Stir in the flour and chocolate until you have a lovely smooth batter. Tip the mix into the prepared loaf tin and bake for 40 minutes, or until an inserted skewer comes out clean.

Remove the cake from the oven, and leave to cool.

FLAPJACKS

 SERVES 4

So simple and cheap. Stop buying cereal and snack bars and start making your own at home. Dried fruit and nuts can be added to this recipe, as well as nut butters. Their inclusion will push the price up but it would make this a more rounded snack. These flapjacks will keep in an airtight container in a cool, dark place for up to a week.

PREP TIME 10 MINUTES
COOKING TIME 25 MINUTES

40g butter
40g brown sugar
50g golden syrup
100g porridge oats

Preheat your oven to 180°C/Gas 4 and line a low-sided baking tray with baking parchment.

Place the butter, sugar and golden syrup into a saucepan over a low heat and melt all the ingredients together, giving them a little stir to help them along.

Tip the oats into a big bowl and pour the melted ingredients over the top. Give everything a good mix together (I use two wooden spoons) and then spread the mix over the prepared baking tray (23 x 15cm).

Bake in the preheated oven for 15 minutes, or until it is just golden brown on top.

Remove from the oven and leave to cool completely before cutting into squares.

SCONES

Scones are one of the best examples of delicious food that doesn't cost the earth to produce. They are sublimely simple, consisting of very few ingredients and can be thrown together by a toddler (under supervision). Once you've got the hang of the plain scone you can begin to experiment with flavours – from toffee and apple to feta and tomato. Go forth and conquer the world of scone!

PREP TIME 10 MINUTES
COOKING TIME 20 MINUTES

450g strong bread flour, plus
   a little extra for dusting
4 tsp baking powder
75g butter, cubed
70g caster sugar
2 eggs
225ml milk, plus a little
   extra for glazing
strawberry jam, to serve
clotted cream, to serve

Preheat the oven to 220°C/Gas 7.

Tip the flour and baking powder into a large bowl and rub in the butter until the mix resembles breadcrumbs. Stir in the sugar.

Beat together the two eggs and the milk until well combined. Work the liquid into the dry mixture until it comes together as a dough.

Tip the dough out on to a lightly floured surface and give it a very light knead, just until you are sure all the ingredients are well mixed. Using a rolling pin, or even the palm of your hand, push the mix out to a thickness of about 2.5cm. Using a 5cm pastry cutter, cut out circles and lay them on to a baking tray. When you are unable to cut out any more circles, bring any of the unused dough together, roll it out again and repeat the cutting process. Continue until you have used all the dough.

Brush the tops of the raw scones with milk and then bake them in the preheated oven for 15–20 minutes, by which time they will have risen and turned golden brown on top.

Let the scones cool a little then cut open, slather with jam and cream and enjoy.

INDEX

A

almonds
  Spiced Meatballs 182
American Feast
  Veggie Burgers with Sweet
    Potato Wedges 149
anchovies
  Bruschetta 191
  Laksa 43
  Panzanella 28
  Patatas Bravas 183
  Prawn Spaghetti with
    Puttanesca Sauce 32
apples
  Apple, Parsnip & Celeriac
    Soup with Chilli Croutons
    122
  Chicken Wings with
    Appleslaw 88
  Mushroom Katsu 160
  sauce 122
  storing 129
aubergines: Thai Basil
    Aubergine 166
avocados 17

B

bacon
  Bacon & Egg Fried Rice 142
  Bacon Tortilla 42
  Baked Kedgeree 66
  Beef Bourguignon 108
  Chicken Provencal 76
  Rich Bean Stew 98
  Twice-cooked Loaded Skins
    50
baked beans: Tex Mex Chilli
    107
Baked Eggs with Sausages &
    Kale 46
Baked Kedgeree 66
baking powder 22
bananas
  Banana & Chocolate Bread 212
  Banana & Chocolate Calzone
    170

Banana Fritters with Toffee
    Sauce 208
  Banoffee Pie 203
  storing 208
Bangers with Cauliflower &
    Butter Bean Mash 92
Banoffee Pie 203
basil
  Pasta Genovese 129
  Thai Basil Aubergine 166
Bean Stew, Rich 98
beans
  Bolognaise Pasties 145
  Bonus Bolognaise 113
  Chorizo & Black Olive Paella
    105
  Smoky Chicken Quesadilla
    40
  see also baked beans; butter
    beans; kidney beans
beansprouts: Laksa 43
beef
  Beef Bourguignon 108
  Beef Stew with Dumplings
    111–12
  Bolognaise Pasties 145
  Bonus Bolognaise 113
  Calabrian Lasagne 106
  Classic Lasagne 114
  Chipotle Steak Wraps with
    Refried Beans 57
  Mini Burgers 187
  Tex Mex Chilli 107
best before dates 15
Blackcurrant Poached Pears
    198
Bolognaise Pasties 145
Bonus Bolognaise 113
Bovril
  Risotto Alla Milanese 125
bread
  Baked Eggs with Sausages &
    Kale 46
  Bread & Butter Pudding 194
  breadcrumbs 194
  Bruschetta 191
  Chappattis 180

Chicken Wings with
    Appleslaw 88
  freezing 18
  freshening 19
  garlic bread 19
  Mega Mushrooms on Toast
    26
  Off Cut Veg Soup 124
  Panzanella 28
  Shakshouka & Flatbreads 31
  Sweet Potato Hash 120
  Tear & Share Bread 118
  Tuna & Tomato Grilled
    Cheese Sandwich 29
breakfast bars 14
British Feast
  Roast Chicken with All the
    Trimmings 152–3
broccoli
  Chicken & Tarragon Pasta
    Bake 136
  creamy sauce 124
  Off Cut Veg Soup 124
  Sardine & Broccoli Linguine
    134
  Sweet Potato Hash 120
Bruschetta 191
bulgur wheat: Spiced Chicken
    & Bulgur Wheat 78
burgers
  Mini Burgers 187
  Veggie Burgers with Sweet
    Potato Wedges 149
butter beans
  Bangers with Cauliflower &
    Butter Bean Mash 92
  Rich Bean Stew 98
butter, freezing 18–19
  Chicken Kievs 80
  Cod Fillets with Garlic Butter
    & Cauliflower Rice 39

C

cabbage
  Chicken Wings with
    Appleslaw 88

cakes & sweet treats
  Banana & Chocolate Bread
    212
  Flapjacks 214
  Fruit & Tea Cake 211
  Scones 215
Cajun Chicken with
  Pomegranate Couscous 82
cannelloni: Spiced Spinach &
  Ricotta Cannelloni 141
capers
  Panzanella 28
  Pork Schnitzel with Potato
    Salad 102
carrots
  Bacon & Egg Fried Rice 142
  Beef Bourguignon 108
  Beef Stew with Dumplings
    111–12
  Bolognaise Pasties 145
  Bonus Bolognaise 113
  Chicken & Leek Pie 71–2
  Classic Lasagne 114
  Egg-fried Rice 173
  Rich Bean Stew 98
  Mushroom Katsu 160
  Pork Chops with Creamy
    Spring Greens & Root
    Mash 101
  Roast Chicken with All the
    Trimmings 152–3
  Spiced Chicken & Bulgur
    Wheat 78
  Tex Mex Chilli 107
  Toad in the Hole with
    Caramelised Onion Gravy
    89–91
  Vegetable Tempura Fritters
    157
  Veggie Burgers with Sweet
    Potato Wedges 149
cauliflower
  Bangers with Cauliflower &
    Butter Bean Mash 92
  Cod Fillets with Garlic Butter
    & Cauliflower Rice 39
  Off Cut Veg Soup 124

  Roasted Cauliflower 181
celery & celeriac
  Apple, Parsnip & Celeriac
    Soup with Chilli Croutons
    122
  Baked Kedgeree 66
  Beef Stew with Dumplings
    111–12
  Bolognaise Pasties 145
  Bonus Bolognaise 113
  Chicken Provencal 76
  Chicken Wings with
    Appleslaw 88
  Chorizo & Black Olive Paella
    105
  Classic Lasagne 114
  crisping 95
  Mushroom Katsu 160
  Rich Bean Stew 98
  Roast Tomato & Orzo Ragu 62
  Sausage & Orzo Ragu 95
  Spiced Chicken & Bulgur
    Wheat 78
  Tex Mex Chilli 107
  Turkey Jambalaya 44
Chappattis 180
Cheese, Luxury Mac & 61
cheese
  Bacon Tortilla 42
  Baked Eggs with Sausages &
    Kale 46
  Chicken & Leek Pie 71–2
  Chorizo & Spinach Frittata 48
  Family Pizza 167
  Luxury Mac & Cheese 61
  Mega Mushrooms on Toast 26
  Pulled Chicken Fajitas 85
  Smoky Chicken
    Quesadilla 40
  Spiced Spinach & Ricotta
    Cannelloni 141
  storing 17, 125
  Twice-cooked Loaded Skins
    50
  see also cream cheese; feta
    cheese; mozzarella
    cheese; Parmesan cheese

Cheesecake, New-York-style
  Yoghurt 207
chicken
  Cajun Chicken with
    Pomegranate Couscous 82
  Chicken & Basil Baked
    Risotto 81
  Chicken Kievs 80
  Chicken & Leek Pie 71–2
  Chicken Provencal 76
  Chicken & Sausage Traybake
    86
  Chicken Stock 121
  Chicken & Sweetcorn Soup
    172
  Chicken Tagine 75
  Chicken & Tarragon Pasta
    Bake 136
  Chicken & Tarragon Risotto
    138
  Chicken Wings with
    Appleslaw 88
  Leftover Chicken Pie
    Croquettes 137
  Family Pizza 167
  Pulled Chicken Fajitas 85
  Roast Chicken with All the
    Trimmings 152–3
  Smoky Chicken Quesadilla
    40
  Spiced Chicken & Bulgur
    Wheat 78
  stock 121
chilli
  Apple, Parsnip & Celeriac
    Soup with Chilli Croutons
    122
  Bacon & Egg Fried Rice 142
  Chipotle Steak Wraps with
    Refried Beans 57
  Crab Stick Fu Yung 36
  Goan Fish Curry 65
  Leftover Chicken Pie
    Croquettes 137
  Pad Thai 164
  Prawn Spaghetti with
    Puttanesca Sauce 32

Thai Basil Aubergine 166
chilli oil 22
Chinese Feast
  Chicken & Sweetcorn Soup
    172
  Egg-fried Rice 173
  Sweet & Sour Pork 174
Chipotle Steak Wraps with
  Refried Beans 57
Chips, Moules Marinières with
  161
chocolate
  Banana & Chocolate Bread
    212
  Banana & Chocolate Calzone
    170
  Churros 204
chorizo
  Chicken & Basil Baked
    Risotto 81
  Chorizo & Black Olive Paella
    105
  Chorizo & Spinach Frittata
    48
  Luxury Mac & Cheese 61
  Shakshouka & Flatbreads 31
  Sweet Potato Hash 120
  Turkey Jambalaya 44
Churros 204
coconut milk
  Laksa 43
Cod Fillets with Garlic Butter
  & Cauliflower Rice 39
coley
  Goan Fish Curry 65
condensed milk
  Banoffee Pie 203
cooked food, freezing 18
cordial
  Blackcurrant Poached Pears
    198
  Lemon Cordial Sorbet 200
cornflakes
  Cajun Chicken with
    Pomegranate Couscous 82
courgettes
  Bacon & Egg Fried Rice 142
  Roast Tomato & Orzo Ragu 62
  Sausage & Orzo Ragu 95
  Thai Basil Aubergine 166
  Vegetable Tempura Fritters
    157

Veggie Burgers with Sweet
  Potato Wedges 149
couscous
  Cajun Chicken with
    Pomegranate Couscous 82
  Chicken Tagine 75
Crab Stick Fu Yung 36
cream
  freezing 101
  Pork Chops with Creamy
    Spring Greens & Root
    Mash 101
cream cheese
  Twice-cooked Loaded Skins
    50
croquettes & fritters
  Banana Fritters with Toffee
    Sauce 208
  Leftover Chicken Pie
    Croquettes 137
  Tuna & Sweetcorn Fritters
    133
  Vegetable Tempura Fritters
    157
croutons: Apple, Parsnip &
  Celeriac Soup with Chilli
  Croutons 122
cucumber
  Cajun Chicken with
    Pomegranate Couscous 82
  Chicken Tagine 75
  Koftas with Chunky Feta
    Salad 55
curry
  Baked Kedgeree 66
  Daal 177
  Goan Fish Curry 65
  Lamb Curry 176
  Mushroom Katsu 160
  Roasted Cauliflower 181

D
Daal 177
dairy products
  freezing 18–19
  storage 17
desserts
  Banana & Chocolate
    Calzone 170
  Banana Fritters with Toffee
    Sauce 208

Banoffee Pie 203
Blackcurrant Poached Pears
  198
Bread & Butter Pudding
  194
Churros 204
Fruitbowl Leftover Lollies 199
Jelly Mountain 202
Lemon Cordial Sorbet 200
Lemon Posset 197
New-York-style Yoghurt
  Cheesecake 207
digestive biscuits
  Banoffee Pie 203
  New-York-style Yoghurt
    Cheesecake 207
Dumplings, Beef Stew
  with 111–12

E
eggs
  Bacon & Egg Fried Rice 142
  Bacon Tortilla 42
  Baked Eggs with Sausages &
    Kale 46
  Baked Kedgeree 66
  Bread & Butter Pudding 194
  Calabrian Lasagne 106
  Chorizo & Spinach Frittata
    48
  Crab Stick Fu Yung 36
  egg whites, freezing 19
  Egg-fried Rice 173
  freshness 207
  Mega Mushrooms on Toast
    26
  Off Cut Veg Soup 124
  Salmon Fishcakes with Easy
    Lemon Hollandaise 131–2
  Shakshouka & Flatbreads 31
  Smoked Haddock & Spinach
    Omelette 35
  Smoked Haddock Fishcakes
    69–70
  Sweet Potato Hash 120
  Toad in the Hole with
    Caramelised Onion Gravy
    89–91
ethnic stores 13

F

Fajitas, Pulled Chicken 85
feta cheese
    Koftas with Chunky Feta
        Salad 55
    Spiced Chicken & Bulgur
        Wheat 78
filo pastry
    Chicken & Leek Pie 71–2
fish
    Fish Tacos with Sweetcorn
        Relish 150
    frozen 150
    Goan Fish Curry 65
    see also individual index entries
fishcakes
    Salmon Fishcakes with Easy
        Lemon Hollandaise 131–2
    Smoked Haddock Fishcakes
        69–70
fish sauce
    Laksa 43
    Pad Thai 164
    Thai Basil Aubergine 166
Flapjacks 214
flatbreads
    Koftas with Chunky Feta
        Salad 55
    Shakshouka & Flatbreads 31
flour 21
food prices 13
freezer management 18–20
French Feast
    Moules Marinières with
        Chips 161
fridge
    cleaning 17
    management 17
fried rice
    Bacon & Egg Fried Rice 142
    Egg-fried Rice 173
fritters
    Banana Fritters with Toffee
        Sauce 208
    Tuna & Sweetcorn Fritters 133
    Vegetable Tempura Fritters
        157
frittatas, omelettes & tortillas
    Bacon Tortilla 42
    Chorizo & Spinach Frittata 48
    Smoked Haddock & Spinach
        Omelette 35

fruit
    freezing 18
    storage 17
    see also individual index entries
Fruitbowl Leftover Lollies 199

G

garam masala
    Apple, Parsnip & Celeriac
        Soup with Chilli Croutons
        122
    Daal 177
    Lamb Curry 176
ginger
    Goan Fish Curry 65
    Korean Pork Rice Bowl 52
    Laksa 43
    peeling 172
    storing 52
golden syrup
    Flapjacks 214
green beans
    Chorizo & Black Olive Paella
        105
    Pasta Genovese 129

H

Haddock Fishcakes, Smoked
    69–70
ham
    Calabrian Lasagne 106
    Panzanella 28
    Tear & Share Bread 118
herbs
    drying 19–20
    freezing 19
    herby garlic oil 22
    pesto 20
    storing 166
hollandaise
    Salmon Fishcakes with Easy
        Lemon Hollandaise 131–2
    Smoked Haddock Fishcakes
        69–70
honey 22
hundreds and thousands
    Jelly Mountain 202

I

ice cream
    Jelly Mountain 202
    storing 19
ice lollies 18, 199
Indian Feast
    Chappattis 180
    Daal 177
    Lamb Curry 176
    Roasted Cauliflower 181

J

jalapenos
    Tex Mex Chilli 107
Jambalaya, Turkey 44
Japanese Feast
    Miso Soup 156
    Mushroom Katsu 160
    Vegetable Tempura Fritters
        157
jasmine rice
    Crab Stick Fu Yung 36
    Korean Pork Rice Bowl 52
Jelly Mountain 202

K

kale: Baked Eggs with
    Sausages & Kale 46
Kedgeree, Baked 66
kidney beans
    Chipotle Steak Wraps with
        Refried Beans 57
    Fish Tacos with Sweetcorn
        Relish 150
    Pulled Chicken Fajitas 85
    Rich Bean Stew 98
    Tex Mex Chilli 107
    Veggie Burgers with Sweet
        Potato Wedges 149
Kids' Feast
    Bruschetta 191
    Mini Burgers 187
    Sausage Rolls 190
Kievs, Chicken 80
Koftas with Chunky Feta
    Salad 55
Korean Pork Rice Bowl 52

L

Laksa 43
lasagne
  Calabrian Lasagne 106
  Classic Lasagne 114
lamb
  Koftas with Chunky
    Feta Salad 55
  Lamb Curry 176
leeks
  Chicken & Basil Baked
    Risotto 81
  Chicken & Leek Pie 71–2
  Chicken & Tarragon Pasta
    Bake 136
  Off Cut Veg Soup 124
lemongrass
  Laksa 43
lemons & limes
  citrus peels 164
  juice, freezing 19
  juicing 134, 197
  Lemon Cordial Sorbet 200
  Lemon Posset 197
lentils
  Chicken Provencal 76
  Daal 177
  Goan Fish Curry 65
lettuce, iceberg
  Korean Pork Rice Bowl 52
  Leftover Chicken Pie
    Croquettes 137
  Pulled Chicken Fajitas 85
Lollies, Fruitbowl Leftover 199
loyalty cards and vouchers 13

M

Mac & Cheese, Luxury 61
macaroni
  Luxury Mac & Cheese 61
markets 13
mascarpone
  Blackcurrant Poached Pears
    198
  Smoked Mackerel
    Tagliatelle 38
mash
  Bangers with Cauliflower
    & Butter Bean Mash 92
  Polenta Mash 186

Pork Chops with Creamy
  Spring Greens & Root
  Mash 101
mayonnaise 17
  Chicken Wings with
    Appleslaw 88
meal planning 12
meat
  freezing 18
  see also individual index entries
meatballs
  Pork & Turkey Sage Meatballs
    96
  Spiced Meatballs 182
Mega Mushrooms on Toast 26
Mexican Feast
  Fish Tacos with Sweetcorn
    Relish 150
milk
  freezing 19
  storing 17
Mini Burgers 187
Miso Soup 156
money-saving tips 12–13
mozzarella cheese
  Calabrian Lasagne 106
  Spiced Spinach & Ricotta
    Cannelloni 141
  Tear & Share Bread 118
  Tuna & Tomato Grilled
    Cheese Sandwich 29
mushrooms
  Baked Eggs with Sausages &
    Kale 46
  Beef Bourguignon 108
  Chicken & Leek Pie 71–2
  Crab Stick Fu Yung 36
  Family Pizza 167
  Mega Mushrooms on Toast
    26
  Mushroom Katsu 160
  Mushroom Risotto 126
  Roast Chicken with All the
    Trimmings 152–3
  storage 26
mussels: Moules Marinières
  with Chips 161

N

New-York-style Yoghurt
  Cheesecake 207
noodles
  Laksa 43
  Pad Thai 164
nutrition 14

O

oats: Flapjacks 214
oils, flavoured 22
  chilli oil 22
  herby garlic oil 22
olive oil 126
olives: Chorizo & Black Olive
  Paella 105
Omelette, Smoked Haddock
  & Spinach 35
Onion Gravy, Toad in the Hole
  with Caramelised 89–91
onions
  onion peelings 65
  storing 66
  Toad in the Hole with
    Caramelised Onion
    Gravy 89–91
  see also red onions; spring
    onions
Orzo Ragu, Roast Tomato & 62
own-brand products 13

P

Pad Thai 164
Paella, Chorizo & Black Olive
  105
Panzanella 28
Parmesan cheese
  Bangers with Cauliflower
    & Butter Bean Mash 92
  Mushroom Risotto 126
  Pasta Genovese 129
  Polenta Mash 186
  Rich Bean Stew 98
  Risotto Alla Milanese 125
parsnips: Apple, Parsnip &
  Celeriac Soup with Chilli
  Croutons 122
passata 106
  Calabrian Lasagne 106

Chipotle Steak Wraps with Refried Beans 57
pasta 19
  Calabrian Lasagne 106
  Chicken & Tarragon Pasta Bake 136
  Classic Lasagne 114
  freezing 19
  Luxury Mac & Cheese 61
  Pasta Genovese 129
  Pork & Turkey Sage Meatballs 96
  Prawn Spaghetti with Puttanesca Sauce 32
  Roast Tomato & Orzo Ragu 62
  Sardine & Broccoli Linguini 134
  Sausage & Orzo Ragu 95
  Smoked Mackerel Tagliatelle 38
  Spiced Spinach & Ricotta Cannelloni 141
Pasties, Bolognaise 145
pastry
  Bolognaise Pasties 145
  Chicken & Leek Pie 71–2
  Sausage Rolls 190
Patatas Bravas 183
pears: Blackcurrant Poached Pears 198
peanuts
  Thai Basil Aubergine 166
peas
  Bacon & Egg Fried Rice 142
  Chorizo & Black Olive Paella 105
  Egg-fried Rice 173
peppers
  Bacon Tortilla 42
  Family Pizza 167
  Shakshouka & Flatbreads 31
  Smoky Chicken Quesadilla 40
  Spiced Meatballs 182
  Sweet & Sour Pork 174
  Sweet Potato Hash 120
  Turkey Jambalaya 44
pesto 20
Pie, Chicken & Leek 71–2
Pizza Feast
  Banana & Chocolate Calzone 170

Family Pizza 167
Polenta Mash 186
Pomegranate Couscous, Cajun Chicken with 82
porcini mushrooms
  Roast Chicken with All the Trimmings 152–153
pork
  Bonus Bolognaise 113
  Calabrian Lasagne 106
  Classic Lasagne 114
  Korean Pork Rice Bowl 52
  Laksa 43
  Pork & Turkey Sage Meatballs 96
  Pork Chops with Creamy Spring Greens & Root Mash 101
  Pork Schnitzel with Potato Salad 102
  Rich Bean Stew 98
  Spiced Meatballs 182
  Sweet & Sour Pork 174
  Thai Basil Aubergine 166
potatoes
  Apple, Parsnip & Celeriac Soup with Chilli Croutons 122
  Bacon Tortilla 42
  Beef Bourguignon 108
  Beef Stew with Dumplings 111–12
  Bolognaise Pasties 145
  Chicken & Sausage Traybake 86
  Chorizo & Spinach Frittata 48
  fried potato skins 137
  Leftover Chicken Pie Croquettes 137
  Moules Marinières with Chips 161
  Off Cut Veg Soup 124
  Pasta Genovese 129
  Patatas Bravas 183
  Pork Schnitzel with Potato Salad 102
  Roast Chicken with All the Trimmings 152–3
  Salmon Fishcakes with Easy Lemon Hollandaise 131–2
  Smoked Haddock Fishcakes 69–70

storing 129
Twice-cooked Loaded Skins 50
Potato Salad, Pork Schnitzel with 102
Prawn Spaghetti with Puttanesca Sauce 32
prawns
  Chorizo & Black Olive Paella 105
  Prawn Spaghetti with Puttanesca Sauce 32
  Smoked Haddock & Spinach Omelette 35
preserved lemons
  Chicken Tagine 75
Provencal, Chicken 76

Q
Quesadilla, Smoky Chicken 40

R
radishes
  Korean Pork Rice Bowl 52
ragu
  Roast Tomato & Orzo Ragu 62
  Sausage & Orzo Ragu 95
raisins & sultanas
  Bread & Butter Pudding 194
  Cajun Chicken with Pomegranate Couscous 82
  Fruit & Tea Cake 211
  Spiced Chicken & Bulgur Wheat 78
  Spiced Meatballs 182
raspberries 17
  Fruitbowl Leftover Lollies 199
ready meals 10, 12
red onions
  Chicken & Sausage Traybake 86
  Chicken Wings with Appleslaw 88
  Chorizo & Black Olive Paella 105
  Family Pizza 167
  Fish Tacos with Sweetcorn Relish 150

Pulled Chicken Fajitas 85
Sardine & Broccoli Linguini 134
Shakshouka & Flatbreads 31
Sweet & Sour Pork 174
Sweet Potato Hash 120
Tear & Share Bread 118
Refried Beans, Chipotle Steak Wraps with 57
Relish, Fish Tacos with Sweetcorn 150
rice 22
  Bacon & Egg Fried Rice 142
  Baked Kedgeree 66
  Chicken & Basil Baked Risotto 81
  Chicken Kievs 80
  Chicken & Tarragon Risotto 138
  Chorizo & Black Olive Paella 105
  Crab Stick Fu Yung 36
  Egg-fried Rice 173
  Korean Pork Rice Bowl 52
  leftover rice, storing 142
  Mushroom Risotto 126
  Risotto Alla Milanese 125
  Tex Mex Chilli 107
  Turkey Jambalaya 44
Rich Bean Stew 98
ricotta: Spiced Spinach & Ricotta Cannelloni 141
risottos
  Chicken & Basil Baked Risotto 81
  Chicken & Tarragon Risotto 138
  Mushroom Risotto 126
  Risotto Alla Milanese 125
Roast Tomato & Orzo Ragu 62

S
saffron
  Chicken & Basil Baked Risotto 81
  Chicken Tagine 75
  Chorizo & Black Olive Paella 105
  Risotto Alla Milanese 125
Sage Meatballs, Pork & Turkey 96

Salmon Fishcakes with Easy Lemon Hollandaise 131–2
Sardine & Broccoli Linguini 134
Sausage & Orzo Ragu 95
Sausage Rolls 190
sausages and sausage meat
  Baked Eggs with Sausages & Kale 46
  Bangers with Cauliflower & Butter Bean Mash 92
  Chicken & Sausage Traybake 86
  Sausage & Orzo Ragu 95
  Sausage Rolls 190
  Toad in the Hole with Caramelised Onion Gravy 89–91
  see also chorizo
Schnitzel with Potato Salad, Pork 102
Scones 215
seafood sticks: Crab Stick Fu Yung 36
serrano ham: Panzanella 28
Shakshouka & Flatbreads 31
shallots
    Prawn Spaghetti with Puttanesca Sauce 32
shiitake mushrooms
    Crab Stick Fu Yung 36
shopping for food 12–13
smoked haddock
  Baked Kedgeree 66
  Smoked Haddock & Spinach Omelette 35
  Smoked Haddock Fishcakes 69–70
Smoked Mackerel Tagliatelle 38
smoothies 18
Sorbet, Lemon Cordial 200
soups
  Apple, Parsnip & Celeriac Soup with Chilli Croutons 122
  Chicken & Sweetcorn Soup 172
  Miso Soup 156
  Off Cut Veg Soup 124
soured cream 107
  Pulled Chicken Fajitas 85

Tex Mex Chilli 107
sourdough
  Mega Mushrooms on Toast 26
soy sauce 21
Spaghetti with Puttanesca Sauce, Prawn 32
Spanish Feast
  Patatas Bravas 183
  Polenta Mash 186
  Spiced Meatballs 182
Spiced Chicken & Bulgur Wheat 78
Spiced Meatballs 182
spices 21, 166
  storing 44
spinach
  Chicken & Sausage Traybake 86
  Chorizo & Spinach Frittata 48
  Chicken & Tarragon Risotto 138
  Crab Stick Fu Yung 36
  Laksa 43
  Off Cut Veg Soup 124
  Smoked Haddock & Spinach Omelette 35
  Smoked Haddock Fishcakes 69–70
  Spiced Spinach & Ricotta Cannelloni 141
  Sweet Potato Hash 120
  Tuna & Tomato Grilled Cheese Sandwich 29
spring greens
  Pork Chops with Creamy Spring Greens & Root Mash 101
  Roast Chicken with All the Trimmings 152–3
spring onions 173
    Crab Stick Fu Yung 36
  Pad Thai 164
Steak Wraps with Refried Beans, Chipotle 57
Stew, Rich Bean 98
stocks
  Chicken Stock 121
  stock cubes 21
store cupboard essentials 21–2
strawberries 17

Fruitbowl Leftover Lollies 199
sultanas
    Bread & Butter Pudding 194
sugar, storing 211, 212
swede
    Bolognaise Pasties 145
    Pork Chops with Creamy
        Spring Greens & Root
        Mash 101
    Toad in the Hole with
        Caramelised Onion Gravy
        89–91
sweet potatoes
    Sweet Potato Hash 120
    Veggie Burgers with Sweet
        Potato Wedges 149
Sweet & Sour Pork 174
sweetcorn
    Chicken & Sweetcorn Soup
        172
    Fish Tacos with Sweetcorn
        Relish 150
    Tuna & Sweetcorn Fritters
        133

T
Tacos with Sweetcorn Relish,
    Fish 150
Tagine, Chicken 75
Tagliatelle, Smoked Mackerel
    38
Tempura Fritters, Vegetable
    157
Tex Mex Chilli 107
Thai Feast
    Pad Thai 164
    Thai Basil Aubergine 166
Toad in the Hole with
    Caramelised Onion Gravy
    89–91
Toffee Sauce, Banana Fritters
    with 208
tofu: Off Cut Veg Soup 124
tomato puree 21, 98
tomatoes
    Bruschetta 191
    Cajun Chicken with
        Pomegranate Couscous 82
    Chicken Provencal 76
    Chicken & Sausage
        Traybake 86

Koftas with Chunky Feta
    Salad 55
Leftover Chicken Pie
    Croquettes 137
Luxury Mac & Cheese 61
Mini Burgers 187
Panzanella 28
Prawn Spaghetti with
    Puttanesca Sauce 32
Roast Tomato & Orzo Ragu 62
storing 76, 82
see also passata
tomatoes, tinned
    Bolognaise Pasties 145
    Bonus Bolognaise 113
    Chorizo & Black Olive Paella
        105
    Classic Lasagne 114
    Family Pizza 167
    Lamb Curry 176
    Patatas Bravas 183
    Pork & Turkey Sage Meatballs
        96
    Pulled Chicken Fajitas 85
    Shakshouka & Flatbreads 31
    Smoked Haddock Fishcakes
        69–70
    Spiced Meatballs 182
    Spiced Spinach & Ricotta
        Cannelloni 141
    Tex Mex Chilli 107
    Tuna & Tomato Grilled
        Cheese Sandwich 29
    Turkey Jambalaya 44
Tortilla, Bacon 42
tortillas
    Chipotle Steak Wraps with
        Refried Beans 57
    Fish Tacos with Sweetcorn
        Relish 150
    Pulled Chicken Fajitas 85
    Smoky Chicken Quesadilla
        40
    Traybake, Chicken & Sausage
        86
tuna
    Tuna & Sweetcorn Fritters
        133
    Tuna & Tomato Grilled
        Cheese Sandwich 29
Tuna & Tomato Grilled Cheese
    Sandwich 29

turkey
    Pork & Turkey Sage
        Meatballs 96
    Tex Mex Chilli 107
    Turkey Jambalaya 44
Twice-cooked Loaded
    Skins 50

U
use by dates 15

V
vanilla extract
    Blackcurrant Poached
        Pears 198
    Bread & Butter Pudding 194
    New York-style Yoghurt
        Cheesecake 207
vegetables
    freezing 20
    vegetable sauce 20
    see also individual index entries
Vegetable Tempura Fritters
    157
vegetarian days 14
Veggie Burgers with Sweet
    Potato Wedges 149

W
Wedges, Sweet Potato: with
    Veggie Burgers 149
Wraps, Chipotle Steak: with
    Refried Beans 57

Y
yoghurt, Greek
    Koftas with Chunky Feta
        Salad 55
Yoghurt Cheesecake,
    New York-style 207

ACKNOWLEDGEMENTS

Many thanks go to the following people who have all helped to make this the beautiful cookbook it is:

Rob Allison, who wrote all the delicious recipes and spent many hours and days conjuring wonderful food out of a fiver's worth of ingredients.

Matt Tebbutt and Susanna Reid, who brightened the *Save Money Good Food* TV Show with their enthusiasm, wisdom and camaraderie.

The wonderful team at Crackit Productions, especially James Kane, Hannah Springham, Nicki Purcell, Louisa Carbin and Elaine Hackett, as well as Camilla Cope from Greenbird Media and Gordon Wise from Curtis Brown.

Publisher Nicky Ross and Claudette Morris from Hodder, and freelance project editor Jo Roberts-Miller.

Emma and Alex, from Smith & Gilmour, who came up with the creative design, worked to an incredibly tight schedule, and were responsible for the art direction at the photography shoot. Thanks also to Pip Spence for her wonderful food styling, Morag Farquhar for her great prop styling and Dan Jones for his beautiful photography.